JOSHUA TREE NATIONAL PARK

MILES

San Jacinto Mtns.

Santa Rosa Mtns.

Palm Springs

Desert Hot Springs

Morongo Valley

Yucca Valley

Joshua Tree Visitor Center

Joshua Tree

Palm Desert

Indio

Coachella Valley

Little

Keys View

Hidden Valley

Indian Cove

Wonderland of Rocks

49 Palms Oasis

Joshua Tree Cultural Center

Twentynine Palms

Mecca

Sheep Pass

Ryan

Geology Tour Rd.

Queen Valley

Jumbo Rocks

White Tank

Belle

Berdoo Canyon Rd.

Hexie Mtns.

Pinkham Canyon Rd.

Pinto Wash Road

Pinto Mtns.

Mojave Desert

Cottonwood Mtns.

Pinto Basin

Black Eagle Mine Rd.

Old Dale Rd.

Cottonwood Visitor Center

Cottonwood

Eagle Mtns.

Sonoran Desert

Coxcomb Mtns.

D0839361

JOSHUA TREE
THE COMPLETE GUIDE

8th Edition

ISBN: 978-1-940754-49-9

Written, Photographed, & Illustrated by James Kaiser

This book would not have been possible without the help of many generous people. Special thanks to Hannah Schwalbe, Kristi Rugg, Lorna Lange, Joe Zarki, Melanie Spoo, Michael Vamstad and the entire staff at Joshua Tree National Park. Additional thanks to Andrea Kaiser, Adam Himoff, Andrea Himoff, Josia Lamberto-Egan, Maria Matijasevic, Bryan Beasley, Grant Thompson, Ryan Johnston, Carrie Petree, Scott Braman, Adam Preskill, and Natalie Stone.

Special thanks to eagle-eyed readers Edward Wilson, Zach Sherman, and Stan Kresowski who spotted errors in previous editions.

As always, a very special thanks to my family & friends, & to all the wonderful people I encountered while working on this guide.

All information in this guide has been exhaustively researched, but names, phone numbers, and other details do change. If you encounter a change or mistake while using this guide, please send an email to james@jameskaiser.com. Your input will improve future editions of this guide.

Printed in the USA

JOSHUA TREE

• THE COMPLETE GUIDE •

8th Edition

A portion of this book's profits will be donated to the
Joshua Tree National Park Association, the primary
non-profit partner of Joshua Tree National Park.

Learn more at joshuatree.org

JAMES KAISER

CONGRATULATIONS!

If you've purchased this book, you're going to Joshua Tree. Perhaps you're already here. If so, you're in one of the most intriguing national parks in America.

Joshua Tree is beautiful. Joshua Tree is grotesque. Joshua Tree is peaceful, crazy, crowded, empty, freezing, sweltering, and a million other contradictions rolled into one. Some people think it's a wasteland. Others love it at first sight. The park lures everyone from elderly wildflower watchers to youthful rock climbers. It's a land of desert adventure packed into a landscape fit for Dr. Seuss—twisted trees and balanced boulders speckling the spectacular scenery. Add a fresh blanket of snow and you might as well be in Whoville.

And now ... my confession: The first time I came to Joshua Tree, I didn't like it. I was camping with friends who invited me on short notice, and we got caught in a winter storm. I had no warm clothes, it was freezing cold, and our fire kept sputtering out. If the park was like Whoville, I was the Grinch, with grouchy complaints flowing from a mouth that was definitely not two sizes too small. On the second night, my friend's puppy, Sadie, woke up in the middle of the night, climbed onto my friend's sleeping bag, and relieved herself on his face. As far as I was concerned, that premeditated piddle made the entire trip worthwhile. But otherwise the trip was a bust. By the time we left, I had little love for Joshua Tree.

Thankfully, I gave the park a second chance. I came back in early spring, when the temperature was mild, and immediately experienced a change of heart. The scenery grew on me. The strange plants fascinated me. But the real revelation came at night, when billions of stars blazed overhead. I was hooked. And I've been hooked ever since. To those of you who have ever gone to Joshua Tree and gotten lost in the stars, this book is for you.

CONTENTS

HISTORY P.99

For thousands of years, Joshua Tree was home to small bands of indigenous tribes. In the late 1800s, gold miners and outlaws arrived. The land was federally protected in 1936, and by the end of the 20th century Joshua Tree had become a famous rock climbing destination.

MOJAVE DESERT P.133

The most popular part of the park, home to fantastic boulder formations and vast Joshua tree forests. Spend a day or two exploring the surreal scenery.

SONORAN DESERT P.203

Characterized by low elevations and high temperatures, this expansive desert seems barren at first, but it's filled with remarkable plants and fascinating sights.

INTRODUCTION

STRADDLING THE BOUNDARY between the Mojave Desert and the Sonoran Desert in Southern California, Joshua Tree is home to some of America's strangest scenery. The park's twisted trees, rugged rock formations, and jumbled geology create a lurid landscape that lures rock climbers, rock stars, and desert aficionados from around the globe.

At roughly 800,000 acres, Joshua Tree occupies a vast chunk of Southern California's desert. But only two major roads run through the park: Park Boulevard and Pinto Basin Road. Park Boulevard passes through the Mojave Desert, which lies above 3,000 feet in elevation. The Mojave has a slightly cooler climate filled with unusual rock formations and thousands of Joshua trees. The rock formations, some as tall as twenty-story buildings, attract a steady stream of rock climbers. Joshua Tree boasts thousands of climbing routes, making it one of North America's premier rock climbing destinations—especially in winter and spring when other vertical playgrounds are covered in snow.

Pinto Basin Road passes through the Sonoran Desert, which is characterized by lower elevations, hotter temperatures, less rainfall, and wide-open spaces. Much of this open space lies within Pinto Basin, a 200-square-mile expanse of land that marks one of the westernmost edges of the Sonoran Desert. Pinto Basin is massive: five of the park's six mountain ranges define its boundaries. Located just a few miles north of sprawling Coachella Valley (one of California's fastest growing areas), Pinto Basin offers a pristine reminder of the rugged beauty of the untouched desert. Joshua trees are absent, but equally fascinating plants such as cholla, ocotillo, and smoke trees call Pinto Basin home.

Thousands of years ago, Pinto Basin was home to prehistoric people. By the time of European colonization, the park was used by the Serrano and Cahuilla tribes. In the mid-1800s, cattle ranchers came to Joshua Tree, followed by gold miners in the 1880s. By the 1920s, the gold was largely gone, the indigenous tribes had been forced out, and only a few hardy white settlers remained. Following the popularization of the automobile, day-trippers from Los Angeles began exploring the desert. In 1936, Joshua Tree National Monument was established, and in 1994 the Desert Protection Act upgraded Joshua Tree to a national park. Today Joshua Tree National Park welcomes over three million visitors each year.

JOSHUA TREE TOP 5

TOP 5 SIGHTS

Hidden Valley, 138
Cholla Cactus Garden, 213
Arch Rock Nature Trail, 207
Desert Queen Ranch, 141
Skull Rock, 183

TOP 5 ADVENTURES

Hiking, 19
Rock Climbing, 23
Biking, 25
Four-Wheel-Driving, 25
Horseback Riding, 25

TOP 5 HIKES

Ryan Mountain, 166
Lost Palms Oasis, 226
49 Palms, 198
Boy Scout Trail, 136
Warren Peak, 194

TOP 5 VIEWPOINTS

Keys View, 158
Ryan Mountain, 166
Warren Peak, 194
Eureka Peak, 197
Mastodon Peak, 224

Mojave Desert

Mojave Mound Cactus

Winter Storm

Ryan Mountain

HIKING & BACKPACKING

JOSHUA TREE IS a desert hiker's paradise. From easy strolls to rugged multi-day backpacks, there's something for everyone. Looking for great views? Joshua Tree boasts half a dozen mountain ranges. Enchanted by lush watering holes? Head to one of Joshua Tree's five desert fan palm oases. Feel like a relaxing walk? Over a dozen short nature trails explore the park's famous scenery.

Hiking is one of the best ways to experience the park. The views from your car are wonderful, but the subtle beauty of the desert is best appreciated on foot. It's hard to enjoy the call of a cactus wren or admire a prickly pear's vivid magenta flowers when you're whizzing by at 35 mph. Venture beyond the pavement, and you will be rewarded.

But before you hit the trail, there are some important things to know. Dehydration is the biggest concern in Joshua Tree. The desert's dry climate robs you of moisture quickly, and there is no drinking water in the heart of the park. Fill water bottles at park visitor centers before venturing into Joshua Tree, and always carry plenty of water on the trail—at least one gallon per person per day when hiking long distances. Sunglasses, sunscreen, and a wide-brimmed hat are essential year-round.

Heat and dehydration are the biggest concerns, but come prepared for a wide range of conditions. Temperature changes of 40°F within 24 hours are not uncommon in the desert. In spring and fall, it's a good idea to pack warm clothes, and in winter jackets and hats are essential. No matter when you hike, be aware of hazards such as abandoned mines, rattlesnakes, and flash floods (p.30).

Most visitors stick to day hikes on established trails, but overnight backpacking is also an option. Roughly 85% of the park is designated wilderness, making Joshua Tree one of Southern California's premier desert backpacking destinations. Backpacking is a great way to avoid crowds and explore remote sections of the park, but it comes with even greater challenges (outlined on the following page). First time Joshua Tree backpackers should stick to the Boy Scout Trail (p.136) or the California Hiking and Riding Trail, which stretches 35 miles from Black Rock to Joshua Tree's North Entrance.

Backpacking in Joshua Tree

REGISTRATION

Backpackers must register at one of the park's 13 backcountry boards. Overnight parking is only allowed at backcountry boards. Visit nps.gov/jotr for details.

WATER

All water sources in the park are reserved for wildlife. You must carry all water for drinking, cooking, and hygiene. Rangers recommend at least one gallon of water per person per day for drinking.

CAMPSITES

Campsites must be located at least one mile from any road and at least 500 feet from any trail or water source. Camping is not allowed in Day Use Areas (indicated at backcountry boards), and camping is not allowed in caves or rock shelters.

CAMPFIRES

Campfires are not allowed in the backcountry.

TRASH/HUMAN WASTE

Pack out all trash. Pack out excrement or bury it in a hole at least six inches deep at least 200 feet from water sources, campsites, and trails. Pack out all toilet paper.

JOSHUA TREE'S BEST HIKES

NATURE TRAILS

Arch Rock Nature Trail

EASY HIKES

Ryan Mountain

MODERATE HIKES

Mastodon Peak

STRENUOUS HIKES

Boy Scout Trail

ROCK CLIMBING

WITH OVER 8,000 known climbs, Joshua Tree is a world-class rock climbing destination. The park's vast array of boulders and rock formations offer endless opportunities for beginners and experts alike. Joshua Tree's proximity to multiple Southwestern cities, combined with its relatively mild climate, lure a steady stream of climbers year-round.

Joshua Tree's first rock climbers arrived in the 1940s, hammering bolts and pitons into the granite. In the 1970s and 80s, as rock climbing grew in popularity, word spread about a strange place in the desert filled with towering rocks. In winter and spring, when snow covered famous destinations like Yosemite, nomadic climbers decamped to Joshua Tree. They blazed challenging new routes, and photos of their exploits graced the pages of climbing magazines. Before long, climbers from around the world were making pilgrimages to "J-Tree."

A comprehensive rock climbing guide is well beyond the scope of this book. If you're looking for good climbing guidebooks, check out the park's bookstores or local outfitters such as Nomad Ventures and Coyote Corner in Joshua Tree. Nomad Ventures also sells the region's most extensive selection of climbing gear. Other great climbing resources are the Friends of Joshua Tree, a private, non-profit climbers association formed in 1991 to represent climbers' interests in the park (friendsofjosh.org).

If you're interested in rock climbing lessons, there are a handful of outfitters that offer private guiding, group lessons, and half-day climbs. Whether you're a beginner looking to learn the ropes or an advanced climber hoping to sharpen your skills, the following outfitters can get you going: Uprising Adventure Guides (joshuatreeuprising.com), Vertical Adventures (vertical-adventures.com), Joshua Tree Rock Climbing School (joshuatreerockclimbing.com), and Stone Adventures (stone-adventures.com).

Though safe when done properly, rock climbing is an inherently dangerous sport. Visitors climb at their own risk in Joshua Tree National Park. In the event of an emergency, call 909-383-5651 or 911. Emergency-only phones are located at the Intersection Rock parking area next to Hidden Valley Campground and at the Ranger Station at Indian Cove.

OTHER ADVENTURES

Biking

Off-road biking is prohibited in Joshua Tree National Park, but there are some good rides on established vehicle roads. Park Boulevard, which runs through the Mojave Desert and passes some of the park's most spectacular scenery, offers Joshua Tree's best paved biking. Joshua Tree's other major paved road, Pinto Basin Road, is more rugged and remote, and the Sonoran Desert scenery is vast and open. There are also a handful of unpaved, four-wheel-drive roads, but they can be sandy in places.

Four-Wheel Drive Roads

Joshua Tree has several rugged dirt roads best suited to four-wheel-drive vehicles. The most popular (and least intimidating) is the 18-mile round-trip Geology Tour Road (p.171). Covington Flats (p.197), which turns off Highway 62 between Indian Cove and Black Rock Canyon, is another good option. If you're really looking to push the limits of your 4x4, check out Berdoo Canyon Road (p.180), Old Dale Road (p.219), or Black Eagle Mine Road (p.219)—and be prepared for some nicks and scratches on your ride. Always stay on established backcountry roads, both for your own protection and for the well-being of the fragile desert ecosystem.

Horseback Riding

There are over 250 miles of equestrian trails and corridors in Joshua Tree National Park. Ryan Campground and Black Rock Campgrounds lie along the 35-mile California Riding and Hiking Trail. Both campgrounds have overnight areas for stock animals. Knob Hill Ranch (knobhillranch.com) offers guided horseback rides in Joshua Tree National Park.

Astronomy in Joshua Tree

Today nearly two-thirds of Americans live where they can no longer see the Milky Way due to "light pollution" (manmade light). But here in Joshua Tree National Park, which boasts some of the darkest skies in Southern California, the Milky Way still blazes across the sky. If you're not looking up at night, you're literally missing half the show. Don't know much about astronomy? Head to Sky's The Limit Observatory (skysthelimit29.org), which holds viewing events throughout the year. The observatory is located just outside the park's North Entrance Station in Twentynine Palms. And if you visit in fall, be sure to check out the Joshua Tree Night Sky Festival, which features workshops, speakers and lots of telescopes aimed at those spectacular stars.

Joshua Tree
BASICS

Getting to Joshua Tree

Joshua Tree National Park is located in Southern California about 120 miles east of Los Angeles, 160 miles southwest of Las Vegas, and 12 miles northeast of Palm Springs. Interstate 10 runs along the park's southern boundary, and Highway 62 (aka 29 Palms Highway) runs along the park's northern boundary, passing through the "High Desert" towns of Morongo Valley, Yucca Valley, Joshua Tree, and Twentynine Palms.

There are three main park entrances: West Entrance, reached from the town of Joshua Tree off Park Boulevard; North Entrance, reached from Twentynine Palms off Utah Trail; and South Entrance, reached from Cottonwood Springs Road off Interstate 10. Three other destinations in the park— Black Rock, Covington Flats, and Indian Cove—are reached by separate roads off Highway 62.

Entrance Fees

A seven-day vehicle pass ($30) admits passengers of one vehicle to the park. There are also weekly passes for motorcycle riders ($25) and individuals entering on foot or bicycle ($15). Frequent visitors can buy an annual pass ($55) or an America The Beautiful Pass ($80), which provides access to all national parks and federal recreation sites for one year.

Visitor Centers

Joshua Tree National Park has three visitor centers, each located near a major park entrance. The most popular, the **Joshua Tree Visitor Center**, is located in the town of Joshua Tree, one block south of Highway 62 on Park Boulevard. The **Joshua Tree Cultural Center** is located at 6533 Freedom Way in Twentynine Palms. **Cottonwood Visitor Center** (p.223) is located at Cottonwood Springs, eight miles north of Interstate 10. **Black Rock Nature Center** (p.193) is located next to Black Rock Campground. Each visitor center has a ranger-staffed help desk, bookstore, exhibits, drinking water, and bathrooms.

When to Visit

Timing is everything if you plan on hiking, rock climbing, or camping in the park. Summers are scorching hot, with daytime highs routinely topping 100°F and nights rarely dipping below 70°F. Winter brings cool days (60°F), freezing nights, and the occasional snowstorm at high elevations. The best time to visit Joshua Tree, weather-wise, is in early spring (March, April) or late fall (October, November), but this is also when the park is most crowded.

Weather

Days in Joshua Tree are typically clear with less than 25 percent humidity. The park receives an average of four inches of rain per year, but that number is only an average—in some years the park gets virtually no rain, in other years several inches can fall in a few hours. Weather in Joshua Tree is wildly unpredictable, so be prepared for anything. Also note that there's generally a 10°F temperature difference between weather reports for Twentynine Palms and the cool, high valleys in the northwest portion of the park.

One Perfect Day in Joshua Tree

Morning - Explore Hidden Valley (p.138)
Late Morning - Hike to Barker Dam (p.145)
Lunch at Crossroads Cafe (p.38)
Afternoon - Ryan Mountain Hike (p.166)
Sunset - Drive to Keys View (p.158)
Dinner at 29 Palms Inn (p.28)

Another Perfect Day in Joshua Tree

Morning - Arch Rock Nature Trail (p.207)
Late Morning - Cholla Cactus Garden (p.213)
Lunch at 29 Palms Inn (p.28)
Afternoon - 49 Palms Oasis Hike (p.198)
Sunset at Eureka Peak (p.197)
Dinner at Pappy & Harriet's (p.38)

Hazards in Joshua Tree

DEHYDRATION AND HEAT-RELATED ILLNESSES

The greatest hazards in Joshua Tree are dehydration and heat-related illnesses such as heat cramps, heat exhaustion, and heat strokes. Drink plenty of water, eat plenty of salty snacks, use plenty of sun protection, and always be aware of your limits in the desert.

ABANDONED MINES

There are nearly 300 abandoned mines in Joshua Tree, many of which contain open shafts and deep tunnels dropping hundreds of feet. Although some mines have been plugged, many remain open. Use extreme caution near old mines.

RATTLESNAKES & SCORPIONS

Both rattlesnakes and scorpions live in the park, but visitors rarely encounter them. Rattlesnakes are not aggressive if left undisturbed, and they go out of their way to avoid people. Scorpions are generally not dangerous unless you are allergic to their venom. Avoid both by watching where you step and keeping your hands and feet out of strange, dark places.

FLASH FLOODS

Flash floods are a legitimate danger anytime it rains. When out and about in Joshua Tree, be sure to avoid canyons and washes whenever it rains or when rain clouds threaten overhead.

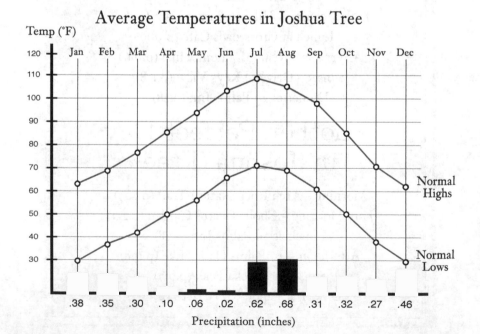

Average Temperatures in Joshua Tree

Hotels & Lodging

There's no lodging in Joshua Tree National Park, but there are dozens of hotels and motels in the towns just outside the park along Highway 62. Rather than wasting reams of paper (when all you need is one hotel room), I've posted all lodging info at jameskaiser.com.

Camping in Joshua Tree

Joshua Tree has nine campgrounds with a total of 490 campsites. Fees range from $15–$25 per night. Most campgrounds require advance reservations, available from recreation.gov. Hidden Valley, Belle, and White Tank Campgrounds are first-come, first-served. Be aware that first-come, first-served campsites are incredibly difficult to obtain during peak season and holiday vacations. Only Black Rock and Cottonwood have running water; you must bring your own water to all other campgrounds. All campsites have fire rings, but you must bring your own wood. See page 32 for campground maps and information.

Camping Outside Joshua Tree

JOSHUA TREE CLIMBERS' RANCH

This private 18-acre campground, located just outside the park and run by the Joshua Tree Climbers Association, offers camping to members of the JTCA or the American Alpine Club. You must be a member to camp here, but membership is free. (climbersranch.com)

JOSHUA TREE LAKE R.V. & CAMPGROUND

This family campground, situated on a small fishing lake, offers hot showers, flush toilets, a laundry room, an RV dump station, off-road access, and a kid's playground. (760-366-1213, jtlake.com)

Organized Activities

RANGER PROGRAMS

Free ranger programs and campfire talks are offered in fall, winter, and spring. Weekly schedules are posted at entrance stations, visitor centers, and on the park's website (nps.gov/jotr)

DESERT INSTITUTE

This adult education program, run by the non-profit Joshua Tree National Park Association, offers a wide range of outdoor courses in the spring and fall. Topics include geology, archaeology, natural history, map and compass skills, desert survival, art courses, and more. JTNPA members receive a 10% discount. (760-367-5535, joshuatree.org/desert-institute)

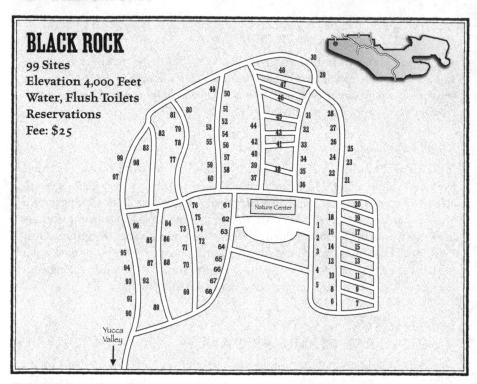

BLACK ROCK

99 Sites
Elevation 4,000 Feet
Water, Flush Toilets
Reservations
Fee: $25

Nature Center

Yucca Valley

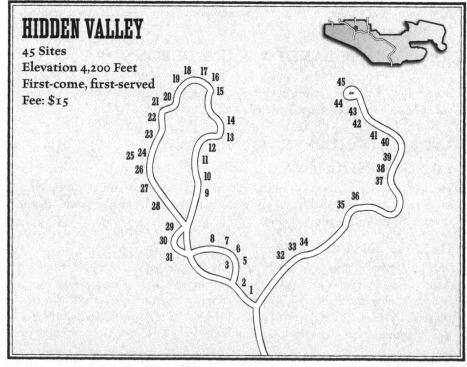

HIDDEN VALLEY

45 Sites
Elevation 4,200 Feet
First-come, first-served
Fee: $15

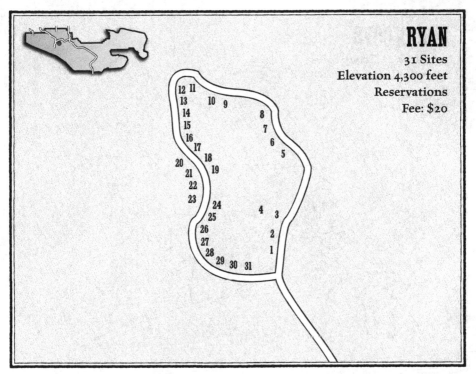

RYAN

31 Sites
Elevation 4,300 feet
Reservations
Fee: $20

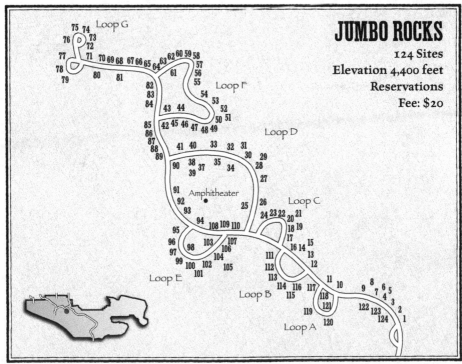

JUMBO ROCKS

124 Sites
Elevation 4,400 feet
Reservations
Fee: $20

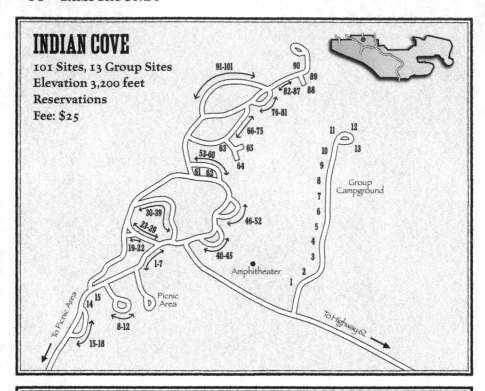

INDIAN COVE

101 Sites, 13 Group Sites
Elevation 3,200 feet
Reservations
Fee: $25

91-101

90
89
82-87   88
76-81
66-75
53-60   63   65
61   62   64
30-39
23-29
19-22
46-52
1-7
40-45
Amphitheater
8-12
15-18
14   15
To Picnic Area
Picnic Area
To Highway 62

11   12
10   13
9
8
7
6
5
4
3
2
1
Group Campground

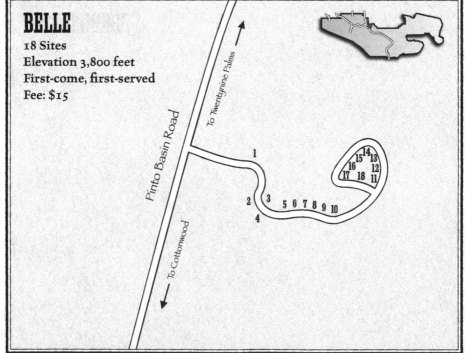

BELLE

18 Sites
Elevation 3,800 feet
First-come, first-served
Fee: $15

To Twentynine Palms
Pinto Basin Road
To Cottonwood

1
2   3   5 6 7 8 9 10
4
14   13
15   12
16   11
17   18

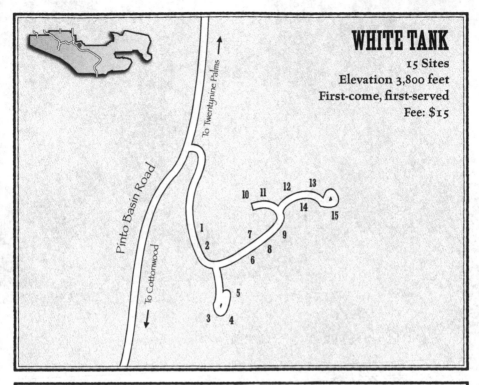

WHITE TANK

15 Sites
Elevation 3,800 feet
First-come, first-served
Fee: $15

To Twentynine Palms

Pinto Basin Road

To Cottonwood

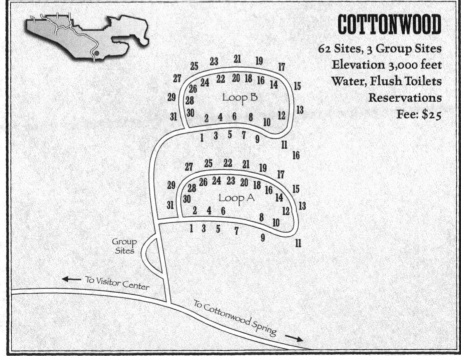

COTTONWOOD

62 Sites, 3 Group Sites
Elevation 3,000 feet
Water, Flush Toilets
Reservations
Fee: $25

Loop B

Loop A

Group
Sites

To Visitor Center

To Cottonwood Spring

GATEWAY TOWNS

THE TOWNS SURROUNDING Joshua Tree National Park are as varied as the landscapes in the park. To the south (in the Sonoran Desert) lies the densely populated Coachella Valley, home to glitzy Palm Springs and countless gated golf course communities. To the north (in the Mojave Desert) are the dusty High Desert towns of Yucca Valley, Joshua Tree, and Twentynine Palms.

For years the towns north of the park conjured images of strip malls, fast food chains, and crew cut Marines. (Twentynine Palms is home to the largest Marine base in the world.) Recently, however, the tiny town of Joshua Tree—sandwiched between Yucca Valley to the west and Twentynine Palms to the east—has undergone a remarkable transformation. Scrappy art galleries, trendy restaurants, and hip Airbnbs sprouted like weeds among the creosotes and cacti. Now a steady stream of L.A. fashionistas make weekend pilgrimages, and rumors of ultra-famous rock stars buying Joshua Tree hideaways abound.

But long before Joshua Tree became hip, the High Desert was a magnet for offbeat personalities. In 1941, Edwin J. Dingle, an Englishman who studied meditation and breathing techniques in 1920s Tibet, founded the Institute For Mentalphysics (now the Joshua Tree Retreat Center) on 420 acres with buildings designed by Frank Lloyd Wright (jtrcc.org). Twelve years later, local resident George Van Tassel supposedly made contact with aliens, an encounter that inspired him to build a giant dome called "The Integratron" (p.44).

Wander the strip malls along Highway 62 and you might wonder if the Integratron was maybe a little *too successful* in luring alien life to the region. Today, the best way to soak in the High Desert's offbeat personality is to explore the shops and restaurants in downtown Joshua Tree. Keep your eyes out for flyers promoting live music and art openings. Or visit in May or October, when the multi-day Joshua Tree Music Festival (joshuatreemusicfestival.com) hosts the region's biggest party.

Clockwise from Top Left: Crossroads Cafe, Joshua Tree Saloon, used cowboy boots, Sacred Sands B&B

Restaurants

Scattered among the postmodern carnage of chain restaurants along 29 Palms Highway are some great, local eateries. The town of Joshua Tree has the most options, but there are some gems in Yucca Valley and 29 Palms.

★CROSSROADS CAFE $$$ (Brk, Lnch, Din)

This Joshua Tree institution serves terrific food in a rustic/industrial Western hipster atmosphere. Breakfast (omelettes, huevos rancheros, polenta & eggs) is served until 2pm. Lunch and dinner feature a wide variety of burgers, sandwiches, salads, and Mexican favorites. (760-366-5414, 61715 29 Palms Highway, Joshua Tree, crossroadscafejtree.com)

★29 PALMS INN RESTAURANT $$$ (Lnch, Din)

Open since 1928, this funky desert inn is home to my favorite restaurant in 29 Palms. Steak, seafood, and pasta are served with fresh veggies (from their own garden), homemade bread, and good wine. (760-367-3505, 73950 Inn Ave, 29 Palms, 29palmsinn.com)

★PAPPY & HARRIET'S $$$ (Lnch, Din)

This old-school honky-tonk serves up tasty cowboy cuisine: Tex-Mex, burgers, great BBQ. Cold beer is served in mason jars, and the live music is consistently good. Reservations recommended on weekends. Closed Tues, Weds. (760-365-5956, 53688 Pioneertown Road, Pioneertown, pappyandharriets.com)

★NATURAL SISTERS CAFE $$$ (Brk, Lnch)

For natural, organic, vegan/vegetarian food, head to Natural Sisters. In addition to wraps, soups, and salads they offer smoothies, fresh juice, and baked goods. One of my favorite places for breakfast. (760-366-3600, 61695 Highway 62, Joshua Tree, thenaturalsisterscafe.com)

ROYAL SIAM RESTAURANT $$$ (Lnch, Din)

This unassuming restaurant serves classic Thai food at reasonable prices. The ambiance isn't exciting, but the food is as spicy as you like on a scale from 1 to 5— and the Chef does not recommend 5! Closed Tues. (760-366-2923, 61599 29 Palms Highway, Joshua Tree)

SAM'S PIZZA & INDIAN FOOD $$$ (Lnch, Din)

Delicious, authentic north Indian food in a strip mall pizza joint? I can't explain it, but I can definitely recommend it. From tandoori to tikka masala, they've got you covered. Sam's also offers pizza, burgers, and subs. (760-366-9511, 61380 29 Palms Highway, Joshua Tree, samsmarketjt.com)

ROADRUNNER GRAB+GO $$$ (Brk, Lnch)

Located next to the Joshua Tree Visitor Center, this tasty deli specializes in grab+go sandwiches, salads, and bowls, plus coffee, tea, snacks, and specialty items. Lots of healthy options. (760-974-9290, 6554 Park Boulevard, Joshua Tree)

COUNTRY KITCHEN $$$ (Brk, Lnch)

For over 20 years this local landmark has been famous for two things: American "Home Cook'n" (eggs, hash browns, country-fried steak) and delicious Cambodian noodle dishes. (760-366-8988, 61768 29 Palms Highway, Joshua Tree)

PIE FOR THE PEOPLE $$$ (Lnch, Din)

Fresh-made New York-style pizza. Customize your pie with a wide selection of toppings (artichokes, prosciutto, Guinness caramelized onions) and sauces (tomato, garlic olive oil, pesto). Calzones, salads and gluten-free pizza are also available. Eat in or call for delivery. (760-366-0400, 58960 Twentynine Palms Hwy, Yucca Valley, pieforthepeoplepizzadicirco.com)

LA CASITA NUEVA $$$ (Lnch, Din)

Twentynine Palms Highway is full of mediocre Mexican restaurants, so it's easy to be let down. If you're craving Mexican, head to La Casita Nueva, which has all the classics: tacos, burritos, enchiladas, plus a large margarita selection. (760-365-5061, 57154 29 Palms Highway, Yucca Valley)

SANTANA'S MEXICAN FOOD $$$ (Brk, Lnch)

This local chain won't win foodie points during daylight, but it's open 24 hours, which means sometimes there's literally nothing better. Overwhelmed by the extensive menu? Try the Chili Verde burrito. (760-366-8297, 61761 29 Palms Highway, Joshua Tree, santanasmxfood.com)

JOSHUA TREE COFFEE COMPANY $$$ (Brk, Lnch)

The best coffee anywhere near the park. Locally roasted, it checks all the sustainable boxes: organic, fair-trade, Rainforest Alliance-certified, solar powered. By the cup or by the bag, this is the best place to get your fix. (760-799-8210, 61738 29 Palms Highway, jtcoffee.com)

FRONTIER CAFÉ $$$ (Brk, Lnch)

Your best bet for reasonably priced, healthy food in Yucca Valley. Located in a beautiful historic building, this funky coffee shop serves tasty sandwiches and salads, plus espresso and tea. (760-365-4100, 55844 29 Palms Hwy, Yucca Valley, cafefrontier.com)

Entertainment

SMITH'S RANCH DRIVE-IN

This drive-in movie theater, which opened in 1954, is a blast from the past: double feature every night, sound track pumped in through your car's stereo system, all under the twinkling desert stars. Even if both films are less than Oscar-caliber (and I've seen some truly forgettable films here), the old-school drive-in experience is unforgettable. (4584 Adobe Road, 760-367-7713, 29drive-in.com)

PAPPY & HARRIET'S

Pappy & Harriet's might be the best honky-tonk in southern California. In addition to the desert's best live music, it offers great BBQ, pool tables, and a rustic country vibe. Located in Pioneertown (p.43), north of Yucca Valley. (760-365-5956, pappyandharriets.com)

JOSHUA TREE SALOON

This local bar (open every day at 8am) is the most popular watering hole in Joshua Tree. Throughout the week there's live-music, open mic nights, karaoke, and trivia. They also offer burgers and tasty food. (760-366-2250, 61835 29 Palms Highway, thejoshuatreesaloon.com)

ART GALLERIES

Joshua Tree is home to a thriving arts community, and local gallery openings are the best place to soak in the scene. Check free local guides (available at stores throughout Joshua Tree) for up-to-date schedules. And don't worry about snobbery—the Joshua Tree art scene is delightfully mellow and friendly.

Outdoor Outfitters

NOMAD VENTURES

This is the best outfitter in Joshua Tree, stocked with a huge selection of climbing gear and climbing guidebooks, plus a good selection of hiking gear, camping gear, guidebooks, and maps. (760-366-4684, 61795 29 Palms Hwy, Joshua Tree)

COYOTE CORNER

This eclectic store offers everything from clothes to books to hot showers. Be sure to say Hi to Ethan, the "mayor" of Joshua Tree! (760-366-9683, 6535 Park Boulevard, Joshua Tree)

Non-Profit Organizations

JOSHUA TREE NATIONAL PARK ASSOCIATION

The park's official non-profit cooperating association. JTNP helps with both preservation and education. (760-367-5525, joshuatree.org)

FRIENDS OF JOSHUA TREE

This rock climbing organization works closely with the National Park Service to preserve the historical tradition of rock climbing in Joshua Tree. (760-366-9699, friendsofjosh.org)

MOJAVE DESERT LAND TRUST

This conservation minded group works to preserve and protect fragile ecosystems in the Joshua Tree region. (760-366-5440, mojavedesertlandtrust.org)

Local Festivals

The **Joshua Tree Music Festival** (joshuatreemusicfestival.com) is a multi-day live music extravaganza held in May and October. The May festival features "an eclectic line up of performers; dance-world-electro-funk'n groove"; the October festival features "artists of the more rootsicana-newgrassy-folkadelic realms." **Bhakti Fest** (bhaktifest.com)—"The premier yoga, sacred music, and personal growth festival in the United States"—hosts Shakti Fest in May and Bhakti Fest West in September. **Contact In The Desert** (contactinthedesert.com)—"The Woodstock of UFOs"—attracts thousands of alien enthusiasts in May. The Desert Stars Festival (desertstarsfestival.com) is another great local music festival.

BEWARE OF YUCCA MAN!

Every region has its Bigfoot legend, and the deserts around Joshua Tree are no exception. Over the past several decades, there have been scattered reports of an unusual creature wandering around the region. Dubbed "Yucca Man," he is the mutant offspring of human parents who abandoned him in the desert shortly after birth. Rather than perish, however, the shaggy infant was adopted by coyotes, who helped him learn to survive in the harsh environment. Today the Wonderland of Rocks is the supposed refuge of this hairy, smelly man-beast. But according to one local skeptic: "There are plenty of unshaven, unwashed, overweight men living [here] who fit that description."

Pioneertown

In 1946, Roy Rogers and a group of Hollywood investors built an outdoor Western movie set near Joshua Tree called Pioneertown. The set's buildings, arranged along a dusty lane, featured a Western-style bank, jail, bathhouse, and saloon. The buildings' interiors offered modern amenities including an ice cream parlor, a bowling alley, and a motel for actors and writers. Today the motel rooms are still available for rent, and the former cantina is Pappy & Harriet's (p.38), a honky tonk famous for great barbecue and live music. To get to Pioneertown, head five miles north on Pioneertown Road off Highway 62 in Yucca Valley.

The Integratron

In 1947 George Van Tassel, an aeronautical engineer who once worked with Howard Hughes, built a small airport in Landers, California, about 10 miles north of Joshua Tree. Six years later, he claimed to make contact with aliens who arrived in Landers from Venus. After inviting him onboard their flying saucer, the aliens entrusted him with a technique for rejuvenating living tissue. Shortly thereafter, Van Tassel and his family constructed The Integratron, a giant dome "located on an intersection of powerful geomagnetic lines that, when focused by the unique geometry of the building will concentrate and amplify the energy required for cell rejuvenation." To cover the cost of construction, Van Tassel hosted UFO conventions that drew tens of thousands of devotees in the 1950s, '60s, and '70s. Although Van Tassel died in 1978, the Integratron's acoustically resonant dome continues to lure a steady stream of musicians, meditation groups, and UFO enthusiasts. Guided tours and "Sound Baths"—a unique relaxation experience where a Sound Therapist plays harmonic frequencies on quartz bowls—are available by appointment. (760-364-3126, integratron.com)

GEOLOGY

JOSHUA TREE'S JUMBLED geology captivates every visitor who sets foot in the park. The scenery is mythical, hallucinatory, and paranormal all at once. Ragged mountains loom above broad valleys filled with twisted Joshua trees. Towering rock formations dot the landscape like giant piles of dripped wax. Alien faces and contorted animals appear in the cracks of rocks. Add some melting watches and Salvador Dalí would feel right at home in Joshua Tree.

You don't need to know anything about geology to enjoy the scenery. But take some time to learn about the forces that sculpted the landscape and you'll look upon Joshua Tree with a fresh set of eyes. As the millennia zoom past the scenery will roll into motion. Mountains rise and fall like sand dunes, Ice Ages blow through like snowstorms, and 100-ton boulders dissolve like sugar cubes.

The story of Joshua Tree's geology begins nearly two billion years ago, when Earth was about half its present age. As eroded sediments washed off ancient continents, sediment accumulated in thick layers offshore. Over time, the deepest layers compressed into sedimentary rock. Then, around one billion years ago, Earth's continents collided to form a single supercontinent called Rodinia. As the continents smashed into one another they crumpled along their edges, forming vast mountain chains. Tectonic collisions generated extreme pressure and heat, and the previously formed sedimentary rock metamorphosed into a metamorphic rock called gneiss (pronounced "nice"). Today this gneiss, which forms the bedrock of many of Joshua Tree's mountains, is the oldest exposed rock in the park. Similar gneiss is found in Australia and Antarctica, suggesting that a chain of mountains once stretched across all three continents when they fused together to form Rodinia.

Around 800 million years ago, Rodinia broke apart. North America drifted toward the equator, and Joshua Tree's gneiss became part of an offshore continental shelf. For the next 250 million years, the landscape that would one day become Joshua Tree National Park lay underwater.

Then, around 280 million years ago, Earth's continents smashed together again, forming the supercontinent Pangaea. Joshua Tree lay off the northwest coast of Pangaea, and sediments once again accumulated in thick layers. When Pangaea broke up around 210 million years ago, North America drifted west and collided with a tectonic plate called the Farallon Plate. The collision pushed Joshua Tree above water and generated intense heat and pressure, exposing the previously formed gneiss to a new round of metamorphism.

As North America pushed west, it overrode the Farallon Plate, pushing the eastern edge of the Farallon Plate deep underground in a process called "subduction." As the Farallon Plate subducted under western North America, it acted like a giant conveyer belt, carrying ocean water deep underground. The friction of the moving plates, combined with Earth's intense interior heat, boiled the ocean water and melted nearby rocks, sending huge pools of magma rising under Southern California. When the magma reached the previously formed gneiss (which, at that point, was buried five to 10 miles underground), it stopped rising and cooled into granite. This granite is called White Tank Monzogranite, and it would ultimately form Joshua Tree's famous rock formations. But it would take one last dramatic act of geology before the rocks attained the surreal shapes we know today.

After the underground granite solidified, it became riddled with millions of cracks. Some of these cracks formed when tectonic forces pushed the granite toward the surface, squeezing the rock from below. Other cracks formed from the compressive weight of the rocks above. Still other cracks formed when surface erosion removed large quantities of rocks above, decreasing downward pressure and causing the granite to expand and crack. These cracks, called "joints" by geologists, formed an elaborate template that would influence the future shape of the rocks.

Over millions of years, as erosion removed overlying rocks, Joshua Tree's crack-riddled granite drew closer to the surface. Eventually, it encountered trickling groundwater, which eroded the granite along its cracks. Granite is composed of feldspar and quartz crystals, and when feldspar comes into contact with water it dissolves into clay. This, in turn, loosens the quartz crystals, which ultimately wash away. Underground erosion sculpted Joshua Tree's granite along its cracks, rounding out the edges and loosening large chunks of rock.

As the years wore on, additional erosion brought the granite to the surface. At that point new forms of erosion, such as freeze-thaw cycles and displacement by plant roots, further shaped the rocks, forming the famous rock outcrops that visitors marvel at today.

A remarkable combination of forces created the fabulous geology in Joshua Tree National Park. Millions of years from now, those same forces will render Joshua Tree completely unrecognizable to modern eyes. So consider yourself lucky. You're alive for that brief moment (geologically speaking) when you can enjoy one of earth's most intriguing landscapes.

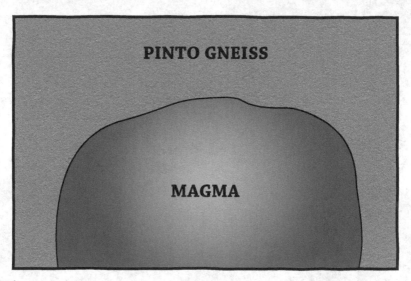

Tens of millions of years ago, giant magma plumes rose under Joshua Tree and intruded on a previously formed rock called Pinto Gneiss. At this point both the magma and the Pinto Gneiss were buried several miles underground.

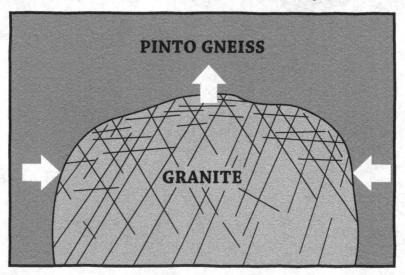

The magma cooled and hardened into granite. As tectonic plates shifted, the granite was exposed to horizontal forces that caused the granite to form vertical and diagonal cracks. Meanwhile, as surface erosion slowly removed miles of overlying rock, vertical pressure on the granite was relieved, causing the previously compressed granite to expand and form horizontal cracks.

Continued erosion of overlying rocks eventually brought the granite close to the surface. The climate of California was much wetter during this time, and as groundwater trickled down it weathered the rock along its cracks.

As Southern California's climate dried out, less water seeped into the ground and weathering of the granite slowed. At the same time, surface vegetation decreased, slowing the rate of new soil formation and increasing the rate of surface erosion. Eventually, the weathered granite was revealed and loose boulders settled into the strange positions you see today.

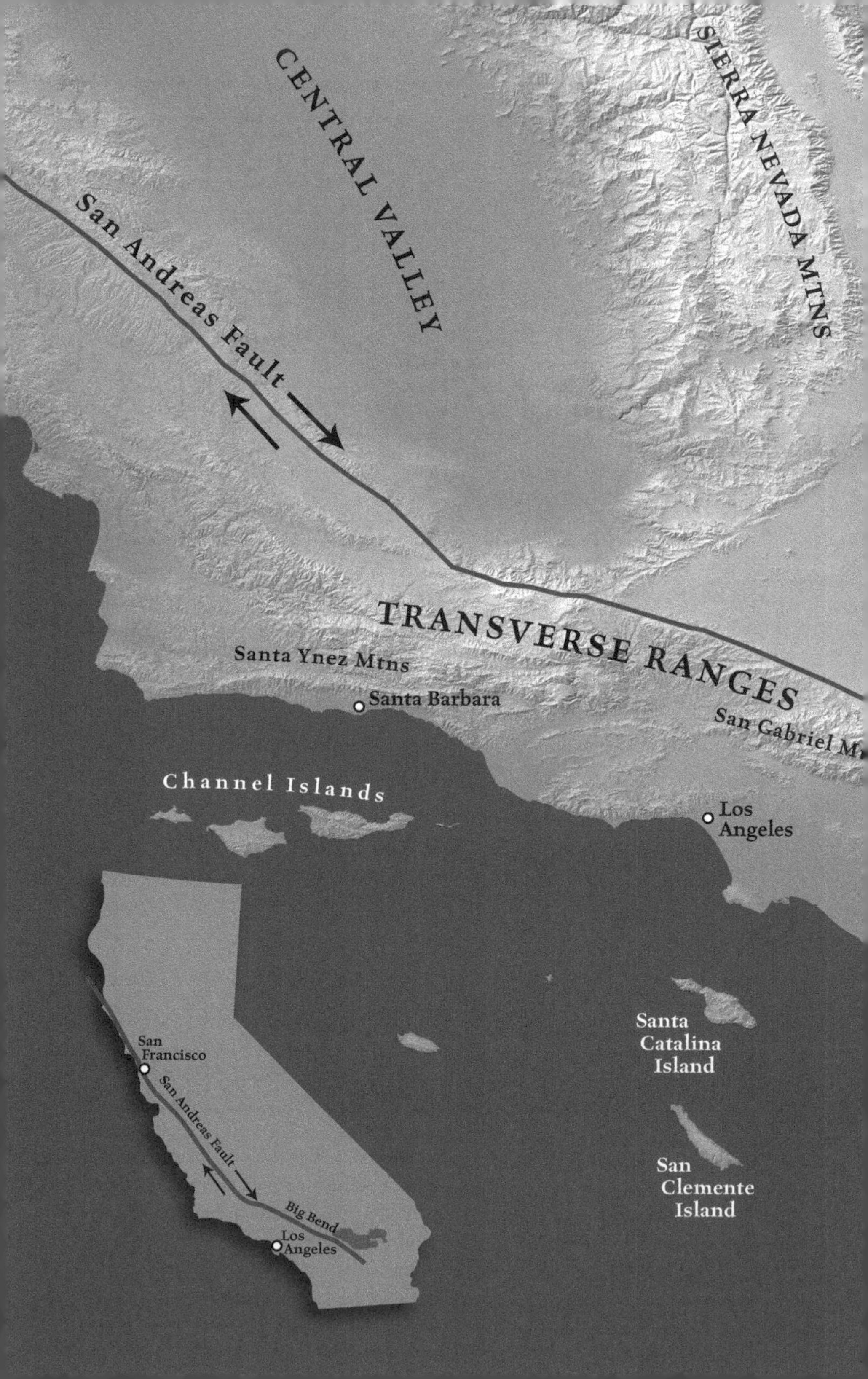

CENTRAL VALLEY

SIERRA NEVADA MTNS

San Andreas Fault

TRANSVERSE RANGES

Santa Ynez Mtns

Santa Barbara

San Gabriel M,

Channel Islands

Los
Angeles

San
Francisco

Santa
Catalina
Island

San Andreas Fault

San
Clemente
Island

Big Bend

Los
Angeles

Transverse Mountain Ranges

This east-west trending mountain system, which stretches from the Eagle Mountains in Joshua Tree to the Pacific Ocean, is a geological oddity. In North America, nearly all mountain ranges trend north-south. The unusual direction of the Transverse Ranges is a result of the San Andreas Fault, which stretches hundreds of miles across California. The fault marks the contact zone between two massive tectonic plates: the North American Plate, which is slowly moving south, and the Pacific Plate, which is slowly moving north. The two plates are generally locked in a stationary position, but as pressure builds they occasionally slip past one another, which triggers earthquakes. Although the San Andreas Fault runs along California in a relatively straight line, it makes a distinct east-west bend in Southern California that concentrates pressure in the region. It is this concentrated pressure that helped squeeze up the east-west Transverse Ranges.

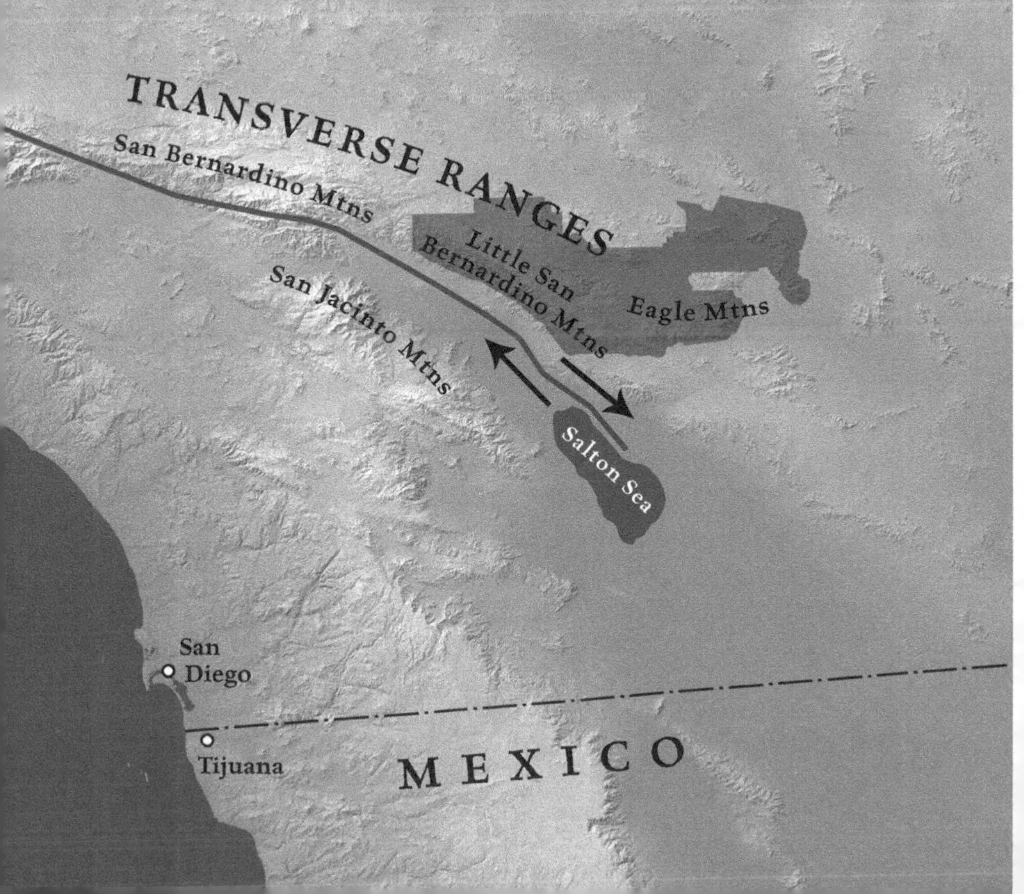

TRANSVERSE RANGES

San Bernardino Mtns

Little San Bernardino Mtns

San Jacinto Mtns

Eagle Mtns

Salton Sea

San Diego

Tijuana

MEXICO

ECOLOGY

STRADDLING THE BOUNDARY between the Mojave and the Sonoran Deserts, Joshua Tree National Park is home to a remarkable range of plants and animals. Although the landscape can seem barren and lifeless, a closer look reveals a thriving ecosystem. Over 50 mammal species, over 40 reptile species, over 250 bird species, and over 800 vascular plant species have been identified in the park.

But life in the desert is never easy. Joshua Tree's plants and animals must contend with an extreme, unforgiving environment. The park's defining characteristic is aridity, which is influenced by a combination of global and local weather patterns. Prevailing winds blow warm, dry air over Southern California, and in Joshua Tree this aridity is compounded by local geography. The park is located at the eastern end of the Transverse Mountain Range, which trends east-west across Southern California. The climate west of these mountains is mild and temperate, but the mountains' eastern slopes descend into some of the most severe deserts in North America. This dramatic transition is called a rain shadow.

Rain shadows occur when mountains wring moisture out of approaching air, creating a dry region on the leeward side. In Southern California coastal air blows east over the region's tall mountains. As the air rises it cools, causing moisture to precipitate as rain or snow. Robbed of its moisture, the air flows down the mountains' eastern slopes bone dry, creating Southern California's eastern deserts. In some places, mountains that are covered in pine trees on their western slopes support just a few desert shrubs on their eastern slopes.

The rain shadow effect is not limited to Southern California. The golden state's nearly continuous wall of north-south trending mountains creates a vast desert region that stretches along much of eastern California. As air flows over these deserts, it passes over additional mountains, which wring additional moisture out of the air. These layered rain shadows extend across much of the American West and northern Mexico, a region sometimes referred to as Aridomerica. This parched region is home to four major deserts: the Mojave, Sonoran, Great Basin, and Chihuahuan. The boundaries of each of these deserts are largely defined by rainfall and elevation.

Great Basin Desert
Salt Lake City
Coast Ranges
Reno
Sacramento
Sierra Nevada
NEVADA
CALIFORNIA
San Francisco
UTAH
ARIZONA
Coast Ranges
Las Vegas
Mojave Desert
Transverse Range
Los Angeles
Palm Springs
Peninsular Range
Phoenix
Sonoran Desert
San Diego
MEXICO
Sea of Cortez
Baja Peninsula
PACIFIC OCEAN

Deserts are sometimes defined as any region that receives less than 10 inches of rain each year. But this vastly oversimplifies the complexities of arid ecosystems. Deserts are more accurately defined by a combination of factors, including low rainfall, high temperatures, dramatic temperatures swings, and a high rate of evaporation.

The western half of Joshua Tree National Park marks the southern tip of the Mojave Desert, which generally lies between 2,000 and 5,000 feet in elevation. On average the Mojave receives three to five inches of rain each year. The Mojave is the smallest of North America's four deserts, covering roughly 50,000 square miles in California, Nevada, and Arizona.

The eastern half of Joshua Tree marks one of the westernmost edges of the Sonoran Desert, which generally lies below 2,000 feet in elevation and experiences searing summer temperatures. The Sonoran Desert covers roughly 86,000 square miles in California, Arizona, and Mexico, including much of the Baja peninsula. In Southern California, the Sonoran Desert is further subdivided into a region called the Colorado Desert, which is bound by the Colorado River to the east. The Colorado Desert is the most arid place in North America.

Joshua Tree is also home to a third ecosystem: pinyon pine and juniper forests growing at the park's highest elevations. This is the only woodland forest in the park, and it offers abundant shelter, shade, and food resources. Pinyon pine nuts provided food for indigenous tribes, and they remain a vital source of calories for many animals.

Mountain rain shadows are a major driver of Joshua Tree's climate, but several additional factors compound the desert's aridity. Because air flowing into the desert is so dry, there's very little cloud cover or plant growth, both of which help deflect the sun's rays. As a result, up to 90 percent of solar radiation reaches the ground. At night, the situation reverses when up to 90 percent of the day's accumulated heat radiates back into the atmosphere through clear, dry skies. In humid areas, by contrast, only about 40 percent of solar radiation reaches the ground, and accumulated heat is often trapped by a blanket of clouds at night.

Because deserts gain and lose so much heat over the course of a day, temperature swings are extreme. Daily highs and lows can vary as much as 50 degrees Fahrenheit. The difference between summertime highs and winter lows can sometimes exceed 100 degrees Fahrenheit.

Southern California's mountains block many winter storms that would otherwise reach Joshua Tree from the west. In late summer, however, storms sometimes blow north from the Sea of Cortez. These storms, which are most common in the Sonoran Desert, tend to be short and violent, sometimes dropping several inches of rain in a few hours. The desert's sunbaked soil struggles to absorb the water, and runoff quickly gathers into deadly flash floods that tear away at the landscape. Despite their damage, these storms are a critical source of water. Joshua Tree's Sonoran Desert receives nearly half of its annual precipitation from summer storms.

DESERT WILDLIFE

The animals that call Joshua Tree home are endlessly fascinating. Some are among the most rugged creatures on Earth. Each species copes with the harsh environment in its own unique way, but they all share a common talent for surviving on limited food and water.

Cold-blooded reptiles are particularly well-suited to the desert. Unable to generate their own body heat, they regulate internal temperatures using the local landscape—basking on sunny rocks to keep warm, retreating to cool hiding places when temperatures soar. Because reptiles burn few calories regulating body heat, they require significantly less food than warm-blooded animals. This is an invaluable adaptation in an ecosystem with limited resources. And unlike mammals, which use large amounts of water cooling themselves through sweating or panting, reptiles use a bare minimum of liquid. Dry, scaly skin helps them prevent water loss through evaporation. Reptiles are such successful water conservationists that many obtain nearly all of their water from food.

Mammals have a much harder time in the desert. Because they must constantly burn calories to regulate their internal body temperature, they require steady sources of food and water. Not surprisingly, mammal densities are relatively low in the desert. Small mammals, which require less food and water, are by far the most abundant. Nearly half of Joshua Tree's mammals are small rodents. To conserve energy, many rodents spend hot days resting in cool burrows, emerging only at night when temperatures drop. Some rodents avoid the sweltering heat of summer entirely by going into a form of seasonal hibernation called *estivation*. Large mammals, by contrast, must always stay close to water supplies. Springs and watering holes are essential for the survival of many of the park's large mammals, most notably bighorn sheep.

Among the most successful desert animals are birds, which can fly between distant food and water sources. Over 250 bird species have been recorded in Joshua Tree National Park, including 78 nesting species. Many of Joshua Tree's migrants visit from nearby mountains, where they spend spring, summer, and fall. Other migrants arrive via the inland portion of the Pacific Flyway, which passes through Joshua Tree. Reliable water sources such as Barker Dam and the park's five palm oasis are some of the places to see birds in the park.

Joshua Tree is also home to an impressive variety of arthropods, including spiders, scorpions, and tarantula hawks. The park is home to over 75 butterfly species, and even more moth species. Aquatic arthropods are among the most fascinating creatures in the park. The delightfully named fairy shrimp is a tiny crustacean that lives in temporary pockets of rainwater. When it rains, dried fairy shrimp eggs rehydrate and hatch. Mature fairy shrimp, which only grow a few millimeters long, splash around for a few glorious weeks before evaporation forces the Joshua Tree pool party to end.

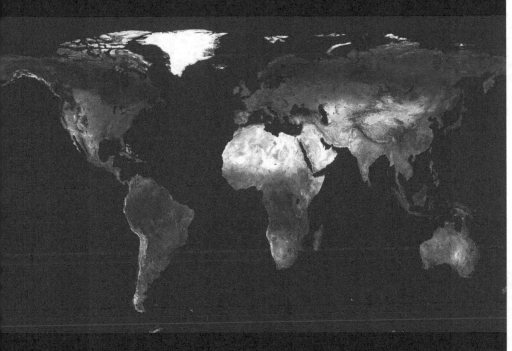

Earth's Deserts

Roughly one-seventh of land on Earth is considered desert. One-seventh! That's an area larger than Europe and Australia combined, with Greenland, Madagascar, and Japan thrown in for good measure. Run your finger across a globe along the Tropic of Cancer or Tropic of Capricorn, and you'll pass over the world's great deserts: the Mojave, Sonoran, Great Basin, Sahara, Gobi, etc. Viewed from space, these deserts form two distinct, dusty brown bands across Earth. Deserts form for a variety of reasons, but their rough alignment with these two latitudes is not a coincidence.

Most of the sun's energy reaches Earth at the equator, heating the land and water and creating vast currents of hot, humid air that rise into the atmosphere. As the air rises, it cools, forcing moisture to precipitate. This creates the regular rainstorms that define the tropics—the lush, wet regions on either side of the equator. Robbed of its moisture, the dry air falls back to Earth near the Tropic of Cancer and the Tropic of Capricorn. The air reheats as it approaches Earth's surface, allowing it to absorb additional moisture. The descending air also creates high pressure zones that divert storms to the north or south. All of these factors combine to create the brown desert bands that stretch across our otherwise green and blue planet.

DESERT PLANTS

Joshua Tree's plants deal with the desert's lack of water in a variety of ingenious ways. Succulents like cacti are water hoarders. Their shallow, extensive root systems gather as much water as possible when it rains. Succulents store water in moist, expandable tissues, and many cacti swell noticeably after it rains. When fully hydrated, succulents can grow for several weeks in dry weather. A few species, like barrel cactus, can survive a year or longer without water. During dry spells, however, these juicy plants become a target of thirsty animals, which is why many cacti are covered in sharp spines.

Other desert plants are drought tolerators, lying dormant for much of the year, then guzzling as much water as possible when it rains. When water is plentiful, drought tolerators photosynthesize and grow rapidly. When dry conditions return, they enter long periods of dormancy. Drought tolerators often have small, waxy leaves that minimize evaporation. In extreme conditions, they can shed their leaves entirely. Some drought tolerators, such as creosote bushes, have deep roots that extend down to the water table.

A third group of desert plants are drought avoiders. Rather than continuously struggle with a lack of water, drought avoiders patiently lie in wait. When it rains they flourish for a few weeks, surviving long enough to produce seeds for the next generation. Drought avoiders are among the most famous plants in the park thanks to their showiest members: wildflowers.

For a few weeks in spring, given the right conditions, wildflowers blanket Joshua Tree in a kaleidoscope of color. But this psychedelic bonanza is never guaranteed. Wildflower blooms only occur following winters with adequate rain. If rainfall is suboptimal, blooms are small or nonexistent. Some wildflower seeds lie dormant for years before rainfall triggers germination. Resinous seed coatings act like natural auto-timers, triggering germination only when there is sufficient water to remove the coating. Resinous coatings also protect against ephemeral rain showers, which would otherwise trick the seed into germinating when there is insufficient water.

Desert wildflowers normally germinate between September and December. But germination does not guarantee a bloom. Warm spring temperatures must follow winter rains for flower stalks to appear. When wildflower blooms occur in Joshua Tree, they often start in February at the park's lowest elevations. As temperatures rise, wildflower blooms spread to progressively higher elevations. Above 5,000 feet, wildflowers can sometimes bloom as late as June. Some of Joshua Tree's best blooms occur during El Niño years, which often bring heavy winter rains to Southern California.

CANTERBURY BELLS

Phacelia campanularia

Tiny blue flowers, 1–1.5 inches, fluted with 5 round lobes at the end. Grows up to 2 feet tall. Found on rocky slopes and sandy washes in the southern Mojave Desert. Following wet winters, thousands of canterbury bells can bloom at a single location.

CHIA

Salvia columbariae

Tiny pale blue flowers bloom from a pointy, globular cluster. Stalks, which grow up to 20 inches tall, can have one or two globular clusters. Chia seeds were harvested by desert Indians. The seeds were eaten, brewed to make a thick beverage, and used for medicinal purposes.

BRITTLEBUSH

Encelia farinosa

Vibrant yellow flowers, 2–3 inches, on branched stalks. Brittlebush is a silvery, gray shrub, 3–5 feet high, covered with small, hairy leaves. The fragrant stems are burned as incense in churches in Baja, Mexico, where brittlebush is called incienso.

DESERT DANDELION

Malacothrix glabrata

Light yellow flowers with a red spot in the center when young. Often grows in large groups in sandy areas. At night, dandelions close and hang like drooping bells. The flowers then reopen in the morning. The name "dandelion" is derived from the French *dents de lion* ("lion's teeth").

DESERT GLOBEMALLOW

Sphaeralcea ambigua

Small shrub with orange, globe-shaped flowers. Stems and leaves are covered with small, star-shaped hairs. Desert Mallow (aka Apricot Mallow) is often found on dry, rocky slopes. The shrub can grow up to 3 feet tall. Globe mallow is a favorite among wildflower watchers.

DESERT MARIGOLD

Baileya multiradiata

Yellow flowers with oblong petals, supported by a narrow stem up to 20 inches. Generally blooms in the spring, but can also bloom after a late summer rain. The name "Marigold" is derived from "Mary's Gold" in honor of the Virgin Mary.

DESERT WILLOW

Chilopsis linearis

Gorgeous orchid-like flowers grow on this tall tree, which reaches 10–20 feet in height. The 2–inch flowers, whitish pink with well-defined purple lines in the throat, grow into thin 7–inch fruits. Found in sandy washes below 5,000 feet where water is available at least part of the year.

BIRDCAGE EVENING PRIMROSE

Oenothera deltoides

Delicate white flowers, 2–3 inches wide, with petals the consistency of tissue paper. Grows close to the ground in sandy terrain. Releases fragrance at night to attract the white-lined sphinx moth. When the flower dies, its stems curl up into a hard globe, often referred to as a "birdcage."

DESERT INDIAN PAINTBRUSH

Castilleja chromosa

Bright red flowers, 1-inch long, bunched at the tip. Often found growing up through other plants and using them for support. Stems grow up to 16 inches tall. Though common throughout the Mojave Desert, its range extends from Southern California to Canada.

DESERT MARIPOSA LILY

Calochortus kennedyi

Vivid orange or vermilion flowers, 1–2 inches wide, with 3 large petals. Grows 4–8 inches tall, often in creosote bush scrub or pinon-juniper woodlands. Mariposa lilies were used as food by Indians, who dug up the bulbs and roasted them. Mariposa is Spanish for "butterfly."

MOJAVE ASTER

Xylorhiza tortifolio

Purple to pale-blue flowers, 2 inches wide, with a brilliant yellow center. Grows 8–24 inches tall, often on rocky hillsides. Mojave aster (aka desert aster) is very common in Joshua tree woodlands between 3,000–5,500 feet.

NOTCH-LEAVED PHACELIA

Phacelia crenulata

Purple to violet-blue flowers, half-inch wide, with five round lobes. Leaves are rounded and hairy. Also called scorpionweed because it can cause a skin rash similar to poison ivy.

SAND BLAZING STAR

Mentzelia involucrata

Sand blazing star produces cream-colored flowers that grow up to 2.5 inches long. The white seeds of its small fruit were an important source of food for native tribes. The seeds were toasted, then ground on a metate, resulting in a food with peanut butter-like consistency.

SAND VERBENA

Abronia villosa

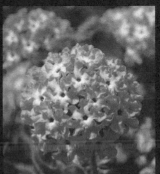

Tiny pinkish-purple flowers. Grows in small clusters that sometimes carpet vast areas. During the day the vibrant colors attract pollinators. At night the flower releases fragrances to attract moths. Flourishes in sandy areas such as dunes or washes.

SILVER CHOLLA

Cylindropuntia echinocarpa

Greenish-yellow flowers. Grows between 1,000 and 5,000 feet. Named silver cholla because of its brilliant white spines. A member of the cactus family, silver cholla produces a small fruit that is said to smell like rancid butter.

WHITE TIDY-TIPS

Layia glandulosa

White flower, 1–1.5 inches, with crisp petals that radiate around a yellow center. A member of the sunflower family. Grows in open sandy soils below 8,000 feet.

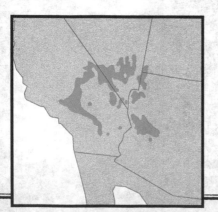

Joshua Tree
Yucca brevifolia

"Grotesque." "Tormented." "The most repulsive tree in the vegetable kingdom." To early European explorers, *Yucca brevifolia* was many unflattering things. But to a small band of Mormons passing through the desert in the 1850s it looked like the prophet Joshua pointing them to the promised land. Although the Mormon's upbeat interpretation was radically different from everyone else's, the name stuck. And it has remained the plant's quixotic epithet ever since.

The Joshua tree has fascinated everyone from 19th-century trapper Jedediah Smith to Irish rockers U2—and with good reason. It's the signature plant of the Mojave Desert. Each tree, tipped with sharp dagger-like leaves, forms a unique profile due to a number of complex environmental factors.

Most Joshua trees grow in the Mojave Desert, but a few stragglers are found in the western Sonoran Desert, southern Great Basin Desert, and 7,000 feet above sea level in the San Bernardino Mountains. There are two subspecies: *Yucca brevifolia brevifolia*, which is larger and grows in the western Mojave, and *Yucca brevifolia jaegeriana*, which is smaller and grows in the eastern Mojave. The largest Joshua trees, some of which reach heights of 40 feet or more, are found in Joshua Tree National Park.

Joshua trees are yuccas that belong to the agave family. Though referred to as trees, their trunks have a fleshy pulp that lacks growth rings. As a result, dating Joshua trees is extremely difficult, but specimens reaching heights of 30 feet or more are thought to be several hundred years old. Although Joshua tree sprouts often grow several inches in their first five years, adult trees grow less than one inch per year after that.

Between February and April, blossoms of creamy greenish flowers appear on the tips of some branches. Blossoming requires a crisp winter freeze followed by adequate rain. Researchers suspect the winter freeze damages the end of the branch, which then stimulates flowering. After a flower appears, the branch splits in two, and when those branches flower they split once again. This random, repetitive branching accounts for the endless variety of Joshua tree shapes. Some Joshua trees never flower and grow completely vertical. As Joshua trees grow, their spiky green leaves die off and fold back, creating a brown woody shag that covers all but the oldest trees.

Like all yuccas, Joshua trees have a symbiotic relationship with the tiny yucca moth. When Joshua trees bloom, a female yucca moth hops from flower to flower, gathering sticky pollen and working it into a tiny ball. She then deposits the pollen ball into a flower's ovaries, fertilizing the Joshua tree. Next, she lays her eggs in the fertilized ovary, and when the eggs hatch they feed on Joshua tree seeds. To ensure a healthy population of Joshua trees, moth larvae only consume about 10 percent of Joshua tree seeds. Yucca moths fertilize Joshua trees, and Joshua trees nourish yucca moths. Charles Darwin called the relationship between yuccas and yucca moths "the most remarkable example of fertilization ever published."

Joshua tree seeds germinate easily, but the nutritious seedlings are savored by ground squirrels, woodrats, and jackrabbits. Seedlings that survive often grow under spiny or spiky "nurse" plants that provide protection during the Joshua tree's fragile early years. Joshua trees also reproduce by sprouting from roots, which allows some trees to survive fires.

Joshua trees, both living and dead, provide habitat for a variety of animals. Scott's Orioles sew basket-shaped nests under Joshua tree leaf clusters. Ladder backed woodpeckers and northern flickers excavate nests in dead, standing Joshua trees. The desert night lizard, North America's smallest reptile, thrives under fallen Joshua tree branches, which attract its favorite food: termites. Desert night lizards, in turn, are preyed upon by spotted night snakes.

In the depths of the Ice Age, 500-pound Shasta ground sloths roamed the Southwest munching on Joshua trees and spreading the seeds in their dung. Then, around 13,000 years ago, humans arrived and the Shasta ground sloth went extinct. The Joshua tree's range has since shrunk by nearly 90%. The Cahuilla call Joshua trees "*hunuvat chiy'a*." They ate roasted Joshua tree fruits and wove the tough leaves into sandals and baskets. Cahuilla weavers prized the Joshua tree's pencil thin roots, which produce a beautiful reddish-brown dye.

Desert Fan Palm
Washingtonia filifera

After Joshua trees, desert fan palms are the most famous trees in the park. The largest palms in North America—and the only palms native to the Western U.S.—desert fan palms can grow over 80 feet tall and weigh up to three tons. But what makes desert fan palms truly remarkable is their ability to survive and thrive in some of the world's most challenging environments.

Despite their propensity for arid places, desert fan palms require a steady water supply. As a result, they generally cluster at spring-fed oases and well-watered canyons. There are just 158 desert fan palm oases scattered throughout southern California, western Arizona, and northern Mexico. Five of those palm oases are located in Joshua Tree National Park. Some, like the Oasis of Mara (p.187) and Cottonwood Springs (p.223), are a short stroll from parking areas. Others, like 49 Palms (p.198) and Lost Palms (p.226), are accessible only by foot, miles from the nearest road.

Desert fan palms have dense mats of pencil-thin roots that extend 20 feet or more in search of water. Vascular bundles in trunks transport water to the top of the tree, where majestic fan-shaped fronds grow up to 10 feet wide. The green fronds live about one year before dying and folding back, forming a shaggy brown skirt, or "petticoat," that is a defining characteristic of desert fan palms.

Fires, floods, and strong winds sometimes remove dead fronds, exposing the brown trunk. Lightning strikes occasionally ignite palms, but natural fire rarely kills mature trees, which are protected

by water-saturated trunks. Fire does kill nearby plants that compete for water, however, so desert fan palms often *increase* seed production following a fire. The largest palms boast thousands of small, round fruits dangling from the crown in dense clusters. The largest palms produce up to 350 pounds of dark fruits, which ripen in autumn and provide abundant food for dozens of animals.

Desert fan palms provide habitat for many species, including great horned owls and western yellow bats. In spring, hooded orioles use thin leaf fibers to weave intricate, basket-like nests that hang under the large fronds. Giant palm boring beetles, which grow up to two inches long, live exclusively in palm oases. Beetle larvae spend years chewing through palm trunks, then emerge as mature beetles through dime-sized holes. Over the next few weeks, giant palm boring beetles mate, lay eggs, and die.

Razor-sharp spines line the edges of desert fan palm leaf stems. Some biologists suspect the spines were an evolutionary defense against Imperial mammoths, which roamed the Southwest during the Pleistocene and grazed on vegetation up to 25 feet high. As luck would have it, when desert fan palms exceed roughly 25 feet in height they stop producing sharp spines.

Native tribes often lived near desert fan palm oases, which provide water, shade, and abundant natural resources. The Cahuilla, Serrano, and Chemehuevi harvested palm fruits using long willow poles. They ate some fruits fresh and sun-dried others, storing them in ceramic jars. Women ground dried fruits into a nutritious flour. Desert tribes used palm leaves to make thatch roofs, clothing, sandals, and baskets.

Far from passive gatherers, desert tribes intentionally planted palm seeds in promising locations. They also set periodic fires in palm oases to clear debris, kill insects, and boost fruit production. Many desert fan palm oases, including some in Joshua Tree National Park, are likely the result of human cultivation. James Cornett, author of *Desert Palm Oases*, believes humans carried desert fan palm seeds north from Mexico's Baja Peninsula, where the palms likely evolved.

European settlers carried desert fan palms even farther. Today they are among the world's most popular ornamental palms, decorating streets in Sydney, Australia and growing alongside the Spanish Steps in Rome.

Pinyon-Juniper Woodlands

Pinyon pines and junipers are two of the most common trees in the West, covering roughly 100 million acres from Oregon to northern Mexico. In Joshua Tree, pinyon-juniper woodlands often occur above 4,000 feet, forming a third, high-elevation ecosystem in addition to the Mojave and Sonoran Deserts.

California Juniper
Juniperus californica

California junipers are easily identified by their stringy bark, scaly green shoots, and tiny blue "berries." Distillers use juniper berries (which are actually tiny pine cones) to give gin its herbal flavor. The word "juniper" is derived from *genever,* the Dutch word for gin. Berries used in gin-making traditionally come from the common juniper, not the California juniper found in Joshua Tree. As the name implies, California junipers grow in California, but their range extends into southern Nevada, western Arizona, and Baja, Mexico. Growing up to 30 feet tall, California junipers send out deep roots in search of water. Tap roots can penetrate 25 feet, while lateral roots spread out 100 feet or more. This impressive root system accounts for up to two-thirds of the tree's total mass, allowing some junipers to grow even after they are toppled over by wind. Under optimal conditions, California junipers can live 1,000 years or more.

Though not as important as pinyon pines to native tribes, juniper trees had many uses. Women fashioned the soft, stringy bark into clothing and baby diapers. Because juniper wood burns evenly with a steady flame, it is considered one of the best woods for cooking fires.

Singleleaf Pinyon Pine
Pinus monophylla

Pinyon pines are one of the most important food sources in the West. Native tribes, modern foragers, and wild animals all enjoy pinyon pine nuts, which are nutritious, delicious, and can be harvested in enormous quantities. Joshua Tree is home to the singleleaf pinyon pine, the only pine tree with just one needle per fascicle. Pinyon pines evolved from Mexican pines around 20 million years ago. As pinyons pines spread north, their nuts became a favorite food of pinyon jays, which gathered nuts by the thousands and buried them for later use. Leftover or forgotten nuts grew into new trees, and over millions of years pinyon nuts evolved new characteristics based on the preferences of pinyon jays. Most pine trees produce small nuts with "wings" that disperse with the wind. Pinyon nuts, by contrast, became large and wingless. Today, pinyon pines are completely dependent on pinyon jays and other animals to spread their seeds away from the tree. When humans arrived in the Southwest, they quickly recognized the nutritional value of pinyon pines. In late summer, when pine nuts ripen, native tribes harvested and stored as many as possible. Some pinyons grow 50 feet or taller, and pine cones on the highest branches were knocked down with long poles. Pine nuts were then roasted, boiled, or ground into flour on stone metates. During harsh winters, an adequate supply of pinyon nuts sometimes meant the difference between life and death. In addition to providing food, pinyon pines produce a sticky pitch that weavers used to waterproof baskets.

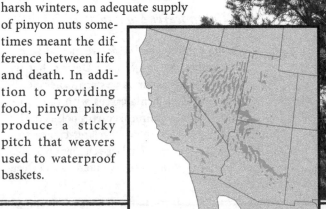

Cacti

These rugged succulents, which first evolved 65 million years ago in South America, are native to the Western Hemisphere. Over two dozen cactus species grow in Joshua Tree National Park. Their nasty reputation for sharp, dangerous spines is tempered by vivid, enchanting flowers.

Pricklypear Cacti

Joshua Tree is home to four pricklypear species, including the famous beavertail pricklypear (below), whose green, spineless pads burst with pink and magenta flowers. Native tribes harvested both the pads and the fruits, which are still eaten in Mexico today. White lumps on some pricklypears are cochineal insects, which attach to the cacti and cover themselves in a sticky white substance for protection. When crushed, the insects produce a dazzling scarlet color rarely found in nature. Aztec rulers cherished clothes stained red with cochineal. Following the conquest of Mexico, dried cochineal became Spain's second-most valuable export after silver. The red dye colored everything from British military uniforms to American flags. Cochineal is still used today as a natural dye in foods and cosmetics under the names "carmine" and "natural red 4."

Mojave Mound Cactus

Echinocereus mojavensis

As its name suggests, Mojave mound cactus is abundant in the Mojave Desert, but its range extends as far as western Colorado. It is the only California cactus with red flowers, and the only California cactus pollinated by hummingbirds. Also known as claret-cup cactus, Mojave mound cactus grows in large clumps up to five feet wide. It often grows on rocky outcrops and steep canyon slopes.

Hedgehog Cactus
Enchinocereus engelmannii

Growing in clumps of up to 15 small cacti, hedgehog cactus boasts some of the showiest flowers in the park. Each cactus supports a brilliant magenta flower, which attracts pollinating bees. Beautiful, multicolored spines inspired the nickname "calico cactus." Hedgehog cactus grows throughout the Mojave and Sonoran Deserts, and it can be found as high as 7,000 feet in the San Bernardino Mountains.

Chollas

Distinguished by cylindrical, branched stems, chollas (pronounced "choyas") are notorious for barbed spines that latch onto fur, fabric, and skin. Detachable cholla stems hitch rides on passing animals, dispersing them throughout the desert. Dropped stems then take root in fertile ground. There are five cholla species in Joshua Tree National Park. The most famous is teddybear cholla (*Cylindropuntia bigelovii*, left), which flourishes at Cholla Cactus Garden (p.213).

Desert Barrel Cactus
Ferocactus cylindraceus

Growing up to 10 feet tall, desert barrel cacti are the largest cacti in the park. Amazing water hoarders, they can absorb several gallons of water during rainstorms, swelling like a balloon. To conserve water, they have a low surface-to-volume ratio that reduces evaporation. A crown of yellow flowers blooms near the top of the cactus, whose small, edible fruits look like mini pineapples. Six-inch spines inspired the plant's genus, *Ferocactus*, which is derived from *ferox*, the Latin word for "fierce."

Creosote Bush

Larrea tridentata

Ranging from California to Texas and covering nearly a quarter of Mexico, the creosote bush is North America's most widespread desert plant. Growing up to 10 feet tall, it has a rounded shape, angular stems, and tiny olive green leaves. In spring and summer, small yellow flowers and fuzzy white seed-balls appear. For millions of years, creosotes lived exclusively in remote Argentinian deserts. Then, roughly 20,000 years ago, they suddenly appeared in North America. It's possible migrating birds carried creosote seeds in their feathers. However they arrived, creosotes had no natural predators in North America, and they spread like wildfire. Creosote roots release toxins and choke off the water supply of surrounding plants, creating barren "dead zones" around each bush. Exceptionally hardy, creosotes can survive temperatures exceeding 120°F and withstand year-long droughts. When faced with severe drought, creosotes shed mature leaves and rely only on newer, smaller leaves, which require less moisture. Creosote leaves are coated with a waxy resin that helps prevent moisture loss and repels animals with its terrible taste. The resin also releases a pungent, medicinal smell. Residents of northern Mexico call creosotes *hediondilla*, "Little Stinker."

Mojave Yucca

Yucca schidigera

Dagger-like leaves, growing up to two feet long, are the defining characteristic of the only yucca species in Joshua Tree. In spring, a tall stalk filled with creamy white flowers rises from the center of the plant. Although sometimes misidentified as small Joshua trees, Mojave yuccas have longer leaves with thread-like fibers that curl along the edges. Indigenous women harvested yucca fibers to weave into ropes, baskets, mats, and sandals. They also roasted the edible fruits and used diced yucca roots and stems for soap and shampoo. Yuccas produce saponin, a natural detergent with anti-bacterial and anti-fungal properties. Today saponin from Mojave yucca is used as a natural foaming agent in root beer.

Sacred Datura
Datura wrightii

These dazzling white flowers grow on sandy roadsides throughout northern Mexico and the Southwest U.S., but they are particularly abundant in Southern California. The petals, which grow up to eight inches long, close into a tight cylinder on hot, sunny days to reduce evaporation and conserve water. At dusk, when temperatures drop, datura petals unfurl into one of the largest flowers in Joshua Tree. At night, large hawk moths with proboscis (tongues) up to one foot long drink datura nectar and pollinate the trumpet-shaped flowers. Sacred datura often bloom in spring, but flowers can appear at any time of year with sufficient rain. The flower emits a foul odor, and all parts of the plant are toxic. But sacred datura is central to the religious ceremonies of many indigenous tribes. All parts of the plant contain hallucinogenic alkaloids that shaman use to induce visions. Datura ceremonies frequently focus on rites of passage, and the visions people experience help determine their future role within the tribe. Even low doses of datura can be fatal, however, so unless you're an indigenous shaman it's best not to try it.

Parry's Nolina
Nolina parryi

This dazzling plant is endemic to California, and Joshua Tree lies in the heart of its relatively small range. In spring, massive flower stalks grow up 10 feet tall and four feet wide. The yellowish, popcorn-like flowers attract pollinating moths and bees. When backlit at sunrise or sunset, nolina flowers appear illuminated from within. When not flowering, Parry's nolina is sometimes confused with Mojave yucca. Both have long, pointed leaves, but Parry's nolina's serrated leaves are longer, narrower, and more flexible. Parry's nolina is the largest of California's four nolina species. It is named in honor of 19th century botanist Charles C. Parry, who documented dozens of plants in the West. Some of the world's most impressive Parry's nolinas grow along Keys View Road in Joshua Tree National Park.

Roadrunner

Geococcyx californianus

These long-legged birds are famously speedy. Although unable to fly more than a few dozen yards, roadrunners can sprint nearly 20 mph on land—the fastest groundspeed of any bird in America. Highly maneuverable, roadrunners use their wings and tail feathers as air rudders, allowing them to brake fast and execute tight turns. Ferocious hunters, their diet includes some of the most dangerous animals in North America, including scorpions, spiders, and snakes. Roadrunners kill rattlesnakes by bashing the snake's head against the ground, breaking its vertebrae. If the snake is too long to swallow whole, a roadrunner swallows whatever it can digest while the rest of the snake dangles from its mouth. Horned lizards are swallowed head-first, with the lizard's horns strategically pointed away from the bird's vital organs. Roadrunners range across the desert Southwest and northern Mexico. Growing up to two feet long, their mottled brown plumage provides excellent camouflage among dusty desert shrubs.

Turkey Vulture

Cathartes aura

Turkey vultures are among the world's most successful scavengers. Six-foot wingspans allow them to ride thermals and soar over vast areas in search of carrion (dead, rotting animals), which they detect with keen eyesight and a powerful sense of smell. Their bald, featherless heads are well-suited to digging in bloody carcasses. The red head and dark plumage, which resemble a turkey, inspired the vulture's common name. Turkey vultures, which are sometimes called buzzards, range from Canada to Argentina and can live 16 years in the wild. The largest turkey vultures live in North America, where adults weigh up to five pounds. Male and female turkey vultures are similar in size and have identical plumage. To stay comfortable in the desert, turkey vultures urinate on their legs, which cools them through evaporation.

Red-tailed Hawk
Buteo jamaicensis

Named for their russet red tail feathers, red-tailed hawks are the most common raptors in the desert. Their shrill, 2- to 3-second scream is instantly recognizable from Hollywood movies, where it's frequently used (inaccurately) for eagles and other birds of prey.

Red-tailed hawks are remarkably agile predators. They are one of the few birds capable of "kiting"—holding still against the wind like a kite on a string. Their eyes are eight times as powerful as human eyes. After spotting prey, they dive-bomb victims at speeds topping 120 mph. Powerful talons exert pressures up to 200 pounds per square inch. Up to 90 percent of their diet is small rodents, but they also eat rabbits, birds, lizards, and snakes. Although sometimes called "chickenhawks," red-tailed hawks rarely prey on chickens. They are, however, one of the top predators of Gambel's quails. Females are about 25 percent heavier than males, weighing up to 4.5 pounds. The largest red-tailed hawks boast wingspans nearly five feet across. Adults live 20 years or more in the wild, and pairs often mate for life. In Joshua Tree National Park red-tailed hawks build large nests on vertical cliff faces and in Joshua trees.

Gambel's Quail
Callipepla gambelii

Ranging across much of the desert Southwest and parts of northern Mexico, these plump birds are often seen wandering in groups, called coveys, of a dozen or more birds. The male's distinctive call—four notes slurred together, rising highest on the second note—keeps a covey together. Gambel's quail is easily identified by its comma-shaped "top knot"—a flamboyant tuft of feathers that sprouts from the top of the head. Males have black faces with white outlines and rusty, copper crowns. Females have bluish gray heads. Mature birds grow up to 11 inches long. Good runners, Gambel's quails spend most of their time on the ground, but they can take flight to escape predators, cross obstacles, or fly to a roost at night. In the heat of summer, they often cluster near water holes. The birds are named after William Gamble, a 19th-century naturalist who explored the Southwest.

Loggerhead Shrike
Lanius ludovicianus

Among the most ferocious hunters in the park, loggerhead shrikes are famous for snatching lizards off the ground and impaling them on the sharp leaves of yuccas and Joshua trees. Bite-sized pieces of the victim are then eaten at leisure. Other prey includes insects, tarantulas, pocket mice, and young ground squirrels. But loggerhead shrikes are not true birds of prey. Unlike raptors, they do not have powerful talons to clutch prey. Loggerhead shrikes are passerines, the order of birds that includes sparrows and finches. "Loggerhead" refers to the shrike's relatively large head.

Cactus Wren
Campylorhynchus brunneicapillus

Growing up to eight inches long, cactus wrens are the largest wrens in North America. Found throughout the desert Southwest, they construct football-shaped nests in thorny plants such as cholla or mesquite, which offer protection from predators. A side entrance in the wren's nest leads to a central chamber. Most of the cactus wren's diet consists of insects and spiders, complemented by fruits and seeds. Both males and females have a brown coloration with spotted white breasts and a white stripe over the eye.

Scott's Oriole
Icterus parisorum

Few birds are as at home in Joshua trees as Scott's oriole. Males have striking yellow and black plumage. Females are greenish-yellow. After spending winter in Mexico and parts of California's Colorado Desert, Scott's orioles migrate to Joshua tree forests each spring. They use yucca fibers to weave basket-shaped nests that dangle under Joshua tree leaves. Parents raise their young in Joshua trees, then return to Mexico in August. Scott's Orioles are named after Winfield Scott, a general in the Mexican-American War.

Hummingbirds

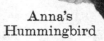

These tiny birds—the smallest in Joshua Tree National Park—are famous for their ability to hover in place and fly backwards. This incredible aerial agility, combined with long slender beaks, helps hummingbirds consume nectar from tubular flowers such as ocotillo and chuparosa. Flapping their wings dozens of times per second, hummingbirds make a distinct humming sound. There are seven species in Joshua Tree, including the only hummingbird species known to breed in the desert: Anna's, Costa's, and black-chinned. Costa's hummingbird is the most desert-adapted species, spending fall, winter, and spring in the Mojave or Sonoran Deserts. Following an elaborate spring courtship, in which males perform 100-foot aerial maneuvers to impress females, Costa's hummingbirds travel to coastal California or Baja, Mexico for the summer. Other hummingbird species in Joshua Tree include calliope, rufous, broad-tailed, and Allen's.

Anna's Hummingbird

Costa's Hummingbird

Owls

There are seven owl species in Joshua Tree National Park, including great-horned owls (left) and burrowing owls (right). Burrowing owls nest in underground tunnels up to ten feet long. The tunnels, which the owls often expand from abandoned tortoise or ground squirrel burrows, keep the birds cool but expose their eggs to predation by rattlesnakes. Burrowing owls compensate by laying twice as many eggs as other owls. Another owl species in Joshua Tree, the diminutive elf owl, is the world's smallest bird of prey. Growing just five inches long, elf owls often weigh just 1.4 ounces. Other species in the park include barn owls, western screech-owls, long-eared owls, and northern saw-whet owls. Owls are nocturnal hunters with excellent night vision and superior hearing. Their distinct facial disk acts like a satellite dish, directing sounds to the ears. Soft feathers with ragged edges enable soundless flight, helping owls launch surprise attacks on small rodents, rabbits, and birds.

Desert Bighorn Sheep

Ovis canadensis nelsoni

Weighing up to 220 pounds, bighorn sheep are among the largest animals in the park. Despite their size, they are exceptionally nimble. Bighorns can navigate steep ledges two inches wide, scramble uphill at 15 mph, and jump down 20-foot inclines with grace. These skills, combined with keen eyesight, excellent hearing, and special concave hooves that grip rocks, help bighorns avoid predators such as mountain lions, coyotes, and bobcats.

Desert bighorn sheep are a subspecies of bighorn sheep native to western North America. Bighorn ancestors migrated from Asia to North American during the Ice Age, then evolved into multiple subspecies. Bighorns in the Sierra Nevada and Rocky Mountains have thick, dark hair that helps keeps them warm. Desert bighorns, by contrast, have short, light-colored hair that helps keeps them cool. Desert bighorns can survive months without water, deriving all of their moisture from grasses, shrubs, cacti, Joshua tree buds, ocotillo, and wildflowers. Like other ruminants, bighorns have four-chambered stomachs that maximize removal of moisture and nutrients. This complex digestive process allows bighorns to quickly gorge on plants, then retreat to high, protected areas to calmly chew their cud.

Both rams (males) and ewes (females) develop horns shortly after birth. Horns grow larger each year, and annual growth rings indicate a bighorn's age. Ewe horns never grow past half curl, but ram horns curve up and over the ears in a dramatic C-shaped curl. A mature ram's horns and skull can weigh 30 pounds and measure more than three feet in length—the largest animal horns in the Western Hemisphere. If horns start to block peripheral vision they are "broomed" (rubbed down) on rocks. During mating season, which starts in late summer, rams battle for dominance. Fights sometimes start with a kick to the scrotum, after which competing rams charge each other

Historic Desert
Bighorn Range

head-on at speeds topping 20 mph. When rams collide their horns smash together, producing a loud crack like a rifle shot that can be heard for miles. Thick skulls allow rams to withstand repeated collisions. Rams can fight for over 24 hours, and aggressive rams with the biggest horns generally do the most mating. Dominant rams may court ewes for days, but mating itself only lasts a few seconds. Although rams are independent by nature, they range between ewe herds during mating season. To mark their presence, rams secrete a scented, waxy substance from the dark preorbital glands in front of their eyes.

Unlike rams, ewes rarely venture far from their natal herd. After mating they carry a lamb for six months, then give birth in spring when vegetation is abundant. Ewes retreat to high, protected areas to give birth, and newborns can walk within an hour. Lactating ewes often gather near water sources to ensure a steady milk supply. During the first months of life, lambs are extremely vulnerable. Fewer than half survive their first summer. Most lambs fall victim to predators such as golden eagles, which swoop down and snatch lambs with their talons. If a bighorn survives its first year, it can often live a decade or more in the wild.

Desert bighorns evolved in a harsh landscape with extreme temperatures. Unlike most mammals, their body temperature can safely fluctuate several degrees, and they can lose over 20% of their body weight to dehydration. (Humans, by contrast, often lose consciousness with a 5% water loss of body weight). In summer, when temperatures soar and plants wither, bighorns gather near water sources. This attracts predators like mountain lions, which patiently wait for bighorns to descend from their steep hiding places to drink.

Up to one million desert bighorn sheep once roamed North America. Native tribes ate bighorn meat, used hides and sinew for clothing, and fashioned bows from their horns. When white settlers arrived in the mid-1800s, bighorn populations plummeted due to diseases transmitted by domestic livestock. Hunting and habitat loss, particularly the loss of reliable water sources, also took a toll. Today, just 30,000 desert bighorn sheep remain. Today government agencies and private organizations, including the Desert Bighorn Council and the Bighorn Institute, are working to increase bighorn populations.

Joshua Tree is home to about 250 desert bighorns that roam the park in three herds. The largest herd, about 120 sheep, lives in the Eagle Mountains. The second-largest herd, about 100 sheep, lives in the Little San Bernardino Mountains. And the smallest herd, which numbers just 30 sheep, lives in the Wonderland of Rocks.

Coyote
Canis latrans

Coyotes are one of Joshua Tree's signature species. Although sometimes elusive during the day, their haunting howls are as common as the stars at night. A long howl calls a pack of coyotes together, at which point a series of high-pitched yips and yelps are added to the mix. These famous vocalizations communicate everything from a coyote's location to their emotional state. Coyote's Latin name, *Canis latrans*, means "barking dog."

The Canidae family, from which coyotes, wolves, and dogs descend, evolved in North America five million years ago. Two million years later, coyotes and wolves diverged from a common ancestor. Historically, coyotes were confined to western North America's deserts and prairies. Following European colonization and the widespread extermination of wolves, coyotes dramatically expanded their range. Today they are found from Alaska to Panama.

Coyotes often travel in packs of six or so closely related family members. Their diet in Joshua Tree consists mostly of small mammals such as mice, squirrels, and cottontails. Coyotes are highly opportunistic, however, eating just about anything, including plants, birds, snakes, insects, and trash. (Despite what you learned on *teevee*, coyotes are not particularly fond of roadrunners.) Working in teams, coyotes sometimes hunt larger animals such as deer and bighorn sheep lambs. While pursuing prey, coyotes reach top speeds of over 40 mph. When lunging, they can jump 13 feet in a single bound.

Strictly monogamous, coyotes mate during the cold winter months. Two months later, mothers give birth to between four and seven pups. When local coyote populations decline, a remarkable adaptation kicks in: remaining coyotes breed at younger ages and produce larger litters—up to 12 pups in some cases.

Coyote fathers help raise the young, supplementing mothers milk with regurgitated stomach contents. Coyote pups open their eyes two weeks after birth. By six weeks they are hunting with mom and dad. But youngsters are extremely vulnerable to predation. Mountain lions and golden eagles prey on coyote pups, and up to two-thirds of young coyotes do not survive to adulthood. Coyotes become independent of their parents around one year of age. Those fortunate enough to reach adulthood often live a decade or more in the wild.

Desert coyotes have special adaptations that help them thrive in arid environments. Weighing roughly 20 pounds, adults are significantly smaller than mountain coyotes, which can weigh 50 pounds or more. Smaller bodies require less food and help dissipate heat. In addition, desert coyotes have shorter, paler fur that keeps them cooler and provides better camouflage. In summer, when the desert sun bakes the landscape, coyotes become strictly nocturnal, spending their days resting in shady burrows.

Coyote plays a starring role in the myths and legends of North American indigenous tribes. No other animal is featured in so many stories. Among a small cast of human and animal characters, Coyote is portrayed as a scheming, meddling trickster that scrapes by on his cunning and charm. The word "coyote" is derived from the Aztec word *cóyotl* (pronounced *COY-yoht*, with a silent *l*). In Aztec culture, coyote symbolized military might, and warriors dressed in coyote costumes. *Huehuecóyotl* ("Venerable Old Coyote") was one of several coyote deities symbolizing music, dance, and carnal pleasure. A noted mischief maker, *Huehuecóyotl* instigated wars among humans as a form of cheap entertainment.

The creation myth of the Cahuilla, who lived in Joshua Tree National Park, places Coyote in a fateful role. When Mukat, the creator, falls ill, Coyote comes to his aide, selfishly hoping to capture some of Mukat's powers. Coyote eventually betrays Mukat and runs off with his heart, dripping sacred blood over the landscape. Coyote then becomes one of the Cahuilla's central mythological characters, helping the tribe adjust to life without Mukat.

When the Spanish colonized North America, coyotes quickly expanded their range, feasting on domestic sheep and goats. European colonists viewed coyotes as a threat, but attempts to exterminate them failed. Intelligent, adaptable animals with a knack for scavenging, coyote populations held steady despite relentless hunting, trapping, and poisoning. When Americans successfully eliminated wolves from much of their range, coyotes happily filled the void. By the 1920s, coyotes had crossed the Mississippi River, and within a few decades they had colonized the Eastern Seaboard. Like their distant ancestors, who roamed the streets of Aztec cities, coyotes thrive in urban environments filled with mice and rodents. Today nearly every city in North America has resident coyote population.

a

Mule Deer

Odocoileus hemionus

Mule deer are named for their large ears, which move independently of one another like the ears of a mule. Common throughout the American West, their range extends from western Canada to central Mexico. In Joshua Tree mule deer are most common at the park's higher elevations.

Mule deer are among the largest animals in Joshua Tree. Does (females) weigh 95 to 200 pounds, while bucks (males) weigh 150 to 300 pounds. Mule deer are slightly larger than white-tailed deer, which do not inhabit the park. Mule deer have white tails with a black tip and bifurcated antlers that "fork" as they grow. White-tailed deer antlers, by contrast, branch from a single main beam. Bucks grow a large pair of antlers each year, then shed them every winter. The annual cycle of antler growth is regulated by seasonal changes in daylight hours.

Male and female mule deer generally avoid each other until mating season in autumn. During the rut, bucks vigorously compete for females. Bucks clash antlers and attempt to force the head of their rival down. Injuries are rare, but antlers sometimes become locked together. If two bucks cannot unlock their antlers, both will eventually die of starvation.

After breeding, males and females separate. Males play no role in raising the young. Gestation lasts roughly 200 days, after which does give birth to one or two fawns. In less than two weeks, fawns can outrun humans. Young fawns have white spots on their back that serve as camouflage. Fawns stay with their mothers roughly five months until they are weaned. Conflict between does is common, so family groups tend to be spaced widely apart. In winter, mule deer migrate to lower, warmer elevations.

Mule deer are ruminants that ferment plant matter in multi-chamber stomachs. They forage on plants, leaves, branches, and brushy vegetation. In summer, when water is scarce, mule deer concentrate near permanent water sources. Adult mule deer sometimes live a decade or more in the wild. In Joshua Tree, mountain lions are mule deer's main predators, but coyotes and bobcats have been known to kill fawns.

Mule Deer Range

Mountain Lion
Felis concolor

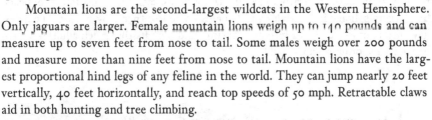

These exceptionally skilled predators (also called cougars, pumas, panthers, and catamounts) are found from Canada to Argentina—the most extensive range of any mammal in the Western Hemisphere. Before European settlement, mountain lions inhabited all 48 lower U.S. states. In the late 1800s and early 1900s, however, they were hunted to the brink of extinction. Following the enactment of strict hunting regulations, mountain lions have made a steady comeback in the West, and they are slowly spreading east.

Mountain lions are the second-largest wildcats in the Western Hemisphere. Only jaguars are larger. Female mountain lions weigh up to 140 pounds and can measure up to seven feet from nose to tail. Some males weigh over 200 pounds and measure more than nine feet from nose to tail. Mountain lions have the largest proportional hind legs of any feline in the world. They can jump nearly 20 feet vertically, 40 feet horizontally, and reach top speeds of 50 mph. Retractable claws aid in both hunting and tree climbing.

Mountain lions travel up to 25 miles a day in search of food, killing prey every four to eight days. Excellent night vision enables them to hunt from dusk till dawn. They are quick, efficient hunters that quietly stalk prey before pouncing. Victims often die from a lethal bite to the spinal cord. In Joshua Tree mountain lions mostly hunt mule deer, but their diet also includes bighorn sheep and smaller mammals.

Solitary and territorial, mountain lions require an extensive home range—up to 400 square miles in the desert. Adult mountain lions come together only to mate. Females are exclusively responsible for parenting, and cubs stay with mothers for roughly two years to learn survival skills. Mountain lion pups are born with spots, but they develop a uniform tan coloration by about 2.5 years in age.

Reclusive by nature, mountain lions go to great lengths to avoid people. Sightings in Joshua Tree are rare, and there has never been a fatal human attack in the park. If you do encounter a mountain lion, slowly back away while holding a steady gaze.

Mountain Lion Range

Bobcat
Lynx rufus

Ranging from the desert Southwest to the swamps of Florida, these highly adaptable felines are North America's most common wildcat. But bobcats are highly elusive and rarely seen. They typically rest during the day and hunt at dusk and dawn. Their diet includes a wide variety of small animals including cottontails, jackrabbits, ground squirrels, and quail. They have also been known to hunt rattlesnakes and young deer. But these stealthy predators rarely chase their prey. Bobcats prefer to seek out a hiding spot and patiently lie in wait. When a victim approaches, the bobcat pounces, snagging its prey with sharp, retractable claws. Bobcats share many personality traits with house cats, including hissing, purring, and using trees as scratching posts. But bobcats, which weigh roughly 20 pounds, are nearly twice the size of house cats. Like most felines bobcats live largely solitary lives. Males and females come together only to mate. Females have litters of two or three kittens in spring, and bobcats that reach adulthood can live a decade or more in the wild.

Desert Kit Fox
Vulpes macrotis arsipusa

Growing less than two feet long and weighing less than five pounds, desert kit foxes are the smallest canines in North America. The have the longest proportional ears of any fox in North America, which helps them detect both predators and prey. Desert kit foxes are nocturnal and rarely seen. Most Joshua Tree sightings occur in Pinto Basin around dusk. Exceptionally well-adapted to arid environments, desert kit foxes obtain nearly all of their water from food. Kangaroo rats, jackrabbits, and cottontails constitute the majority of their diet, but kit foxes also eat birds, reptiles, and insects. Coyotes are the desert kit fox's only known predator. When pursued by coyotes, desert kit foxes can run up to 25 mph.

Ringtail Cat
Bassariscus astutus

One of the park's most elusive and adorable mammals, ringtail cats have big eyes, diminutive faces, and long, fluffy tails. Although they have many feline characteristics—agility, semi-retractable claws, impressive climbing skills—they are not technically cats. They belong to the procyonid family, which includes raccoons, coatis, and kinkajous. Legend has it that miners kept ringtails as pets to hunt mice and rodents. This resulted in the colloquial name "miners cat," which later became "ringtail cat." Ringtails measure roughly two feet long, about half of which is their black-and-white tail. Nocturnal hunters with excellent night vision, ringtails are omnivores that eat rodents, lizards, berries, and fruits. Predators include owls, hawks, and bobcats, but ringtails are excellent at avoiding predation. When threatened they release a foul-smelling secretion. Though rarely seen, ringtail cats range across the desert Southwest and northern Mexico.

American Badger
Taxidea taxus

Badgers are rarely seen in Joshua Tree, but these stout predators strike fear into the hearts of small rodents. Long claws and powerful forearms help badgers penetrate burrows, snatching their favorite delicacies. Badgers also prey on ground-nesting birds, lizards, and rattlesnakes. Interestingly, badgers sometimes hunt with coyotes. After the coyote chases a rodent into its burrow, the badger digs it out. Working together, the pair increases its chance of success. The American badger, which ranges from central Canada to southern Mexico, is the only badger species in the Western Hemisphere. It grows up to 30 inches long and can live 10 or more years in the wild. Joshua Tree is home to the American badger subspecies *Taxidea taxus berlandieri*, which is found in the U.S. southwest and northern Mexico. This desert subspecies is distinguished by a white head stripe that stretches across the back to the base of the tail.

Bats

There are 16 bat species in Joshua Tree, including the California leaf-nosed bat (*Macrotus californicus*), above, and the Western mastiff (*Eumops perotis*), which has a nearly two-foot wingspan. Most desert bats are insectivores, using echolocation to hunt enormous quantities of moths, mosquitoes, and beetles. One Joshua Tree species, the pallid bat (*Antrozous pallidus*) is also able to eat scorpions. Bats roost in rock crevices, trees, caves, and abandoned mine shafts. In Joshua Tree National Park, up to 90% of bat foraging occurs in desert washes.

Kangaroo Rats

Named for their powerful hind legs, which propel them up to 10 feet in a single hop, kangaroo rats are among nature's most water-efficient mammals. They can manufacture water metabolically from dry seeds, and their kidneys concentrate urine up to 20 times. Long nasal passages condense and retain moisture during exhalation. Many kangaroo rats go their entire lives without drinking water. During the day, when temperatures soar, kangaroo rats rest in cool burrows. At night, when temperatures drop, they forage for seeds. To escape predators, kangaroo rats have breakaway tails that detach when grabbed.

Woodrats

Woodrats, also called packrats, are one of the few desert rodents active during the day. Although far less water efficient than kangaroo rats, woodrats are the only rodent species capable of eating cacti and succulents. They are nimble enough to avoid sharp spines, and their digestive system can metabolize oxalic acid, a chemical in cacti that causes kidney damage in other animals. Woodrats are famous for their middens: large debris piles built over many generations. When woodrats urinate on middens, they crystallize the contents in an amber-like matrix, preserving them for thousands of years. Ancient middens offer modern-day scientists an unparalleled glimpse of prehistoric plant and animal matter gathered by woodrats.

Black-tailed Jackrabbit
Lepus californicus

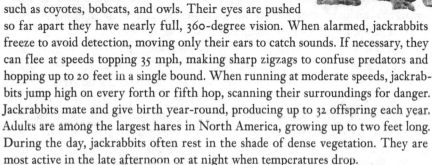

Jackrabbits are one of Joshua Tree's most commonly encountered mammals. Found throughout the West, they were originally called "jackass rabbits" because their enormous ears reminded settlers of donkey ears. Jackrabbit ears account for 20% of their body surface, which not only gives them exceptional hearing but also helps dissipate excess heat through capillaries. Jackrabbits have highly advanced senses and reflexes to avoid predators such as coyotes, bobcats, and owls. Their eyes are pushed so far apart they have nearly full, 360-degree vision. When alarmed, jackrabbits freeze to avoid detection, moving only their ears to catch sounds. If necessary, they can flee at speeds topping 35 mph, making sharp zigzags to confuse predators and hopping up to 20 feet in a single bound. When running at moderate speeds, jackrabbits jump high on every forth or fifth hop, scanning their surroundings for danger. Jackrabbits mate and give birth year-round, producing up to 32 offspring each year. Adults are among the largest hares in North America, growing up to two feet long. During the day, jackrabbits often rest in the shade of dense vegetation. They are most active in the late afternoon or at night when temperatures drop.

Desert Cottontail
Sylvilagus audubonii

Named for their puffy white tails, desert cottontails range from eastern Montana to central Mexico. Adults grow up to 17 inches long and weigh up to 3.3 pounds. Strict vegetarians, desert cottontails feed primarily on grasses, but during severe droughts they also eat cacti. Like most rabbits, cottontails re-ingest their own feces to extract maximum nutrition from food. Desert cottontails are most active in the early morning and late afternoon. During the heat of the day, they rest in shady burrows, which are often dug by other rodents and later occupied by cottontails. Predators include coyotes, bobcats, and mountain lions. Due to their high reproductive rate (up to 30 young per year) and relative abundance, desert cottontails were an important resource for indigenous tribes. Both the Cahuilla and Serrano ate cottontail meat and used their soft pelts to make warm blankets.

Desert Tortoise

Gopherus agassizii

Weighing up to 50 pounds, desert tortoises are the largest reptiles in Joshua Tree. Although rarely seen, they are one of the park's most fascinating creatures. Their remarkable biology, combined with a troubling population decline, make desert tortoises one of the park's most-studied animals.

To conserve water and energy, desert tortoises spend up to 95 percent of their time underground. They are arguably the most highly evolved burrowers of any tortoise species. Long claws and powerful legs help tortoises dig burrows up to 30 feet long. Although most burrows shelter a lone individual, 17 desert tortoises were once discovered sharing a single burrow. Underground burrows are cool in summer and warm in winter, when freezing temperatures can be deadly. To conserve energy in winter, desert tortoises hibernate three to six months.

The end of hibernation generally coincides with desert wildflower blooms, which are all-you-can-eat buffets for tortoises. Fresh flowers, leaves, and stems help tortoises replenish depleted water and nutrients. Tortoises are extremely active during this time, consuming up to four percent of their body weight in flowers each day. Those fortunate enough to find water can drink up to 40% of their body weight. Special organs, including an immense bladder, allow tortoises to store water for up to one year, helping them survive prolonged droughts.

Most desert tortoises live in the Mojave and Sonoran deserts, but their range extends as far south as the tropical deciduous forest of Sinaloa, Mexico. Although desert tortoises can live up to a century, they rarely wander more than a few miles from their birthplace. Their maximum speed is just 0.2 miles per hour.

When male tortoises meet, things often get ornery. Territory, including any females living there, is fiercely defended. Males repeatedly ram each other with their gular horn, a hard protrusion extending from the underside of the front shell. The battle ends when one tortoise is flipped upside down. Most overturned tortoises are able to right themselves, but those that can't sometimes die of exposure or starvation.

Mojave Desert
Tortoise Range

When a male tortoise encounters a female it almost always tries to mate. After approaching a female head-on, the male bites at her legs and face. The female withdraws into her shell, at which point the male rams her with his gular horn. He then mounts her from behind, standing in a nearly vertical position. After few minutes of thrusting, he leaves. Females can retain sperm for up to ten years and still lay eggs. When a female is ready, she digs a hole in the ground and lays up to a dozen ping pong ball-sized eggs. She then covers the hole and urinates on it (perhaps to mask the scent or humidify the site). The eggs hatch roughly three months later.

Tortoise hatchlings, which measure just two inches long, are extremely vulnerable to predation by ravens, kit foxes, and other animals. Because tortoise shells don't fully harden for five years, juveniles remain vulnerable to golden eagles, coyotes, and mountain lions. It's estimated that less than two percent of desert tortoise hatchlings survive to adulthood. Those that do enjoy a hard, protective shell that measures up to 14 inches long. When threatened, adult tortoises withdraw their head and limbs into their shell, comfortably waiting out predators for hours or even days. Tortoise shells are comprised of interlocking plates, called scutes, that have annual growth rings like trees.

Desert tortoises were an important resource for indigenous tribes, particularly during droughts when other animals were scarce. Because tortoises can survive for long periods without food and water, they were often kept alive in corrals until needed. The Cahuilla roasted tortoises over open fires, eating the meat and using the shells to make spoons, ladles, and bowls.

In the remote western Mojave Desert, tortoise densities can reach up to four hundred individuals per square mile. Throughout much of their range, however, densities are significantly lower. Over the past century, as modern man colonized the Southwest, desert tortoise populations declined due to habitat loss, diseases spread by pet turtles, speeding vehicles, and predators such as ravens that thrive alongside humans. Because desert tortoises don't reach sexual maturity until at least 15 years of age, even small population declines can have devastating impacts. In 1989, desert tortoises were placed on the California Endangered Species List. The following year they were places on the Federal Endangered Species List.

If you encounter a desert tortoise in the park, do not disturb it. Tortoises empty their bladders when frightened, robbing them of a critical water source. In addition, handling wild tortoises is illegal under the Endangered Species Act. Only if a tortoise is on a road and in danger of being struck by a vehicle should it be picked up and moved out of harms way. Watch out for tortoises when driving, and always check under your car before leaving a parking space. Desert tortoises sometimes seek shade under parked cars on hot days.

Snakes

Western Diamondback

There are over two dozen snake species in Joshua Tree, but sightings are relatively rare because these cold-blooded reptiles go out of their way to avoid people. Many snakes are nocturnal, and most enter a hibernation-like state during the cold winter months. Snakes are generally most active in spring, when warm temperatures lure them out of their dens to mate.

Joshua Tree is home to seven rattlesnake species. They include the eight-foot western diamondback (*Crotalus atrox*), the largest rattlesnake in the West, and the Mojave rattlesnake (*Crotalus cerastes*), which has one of the most toxic venoms in North America. Two Joshua Tree rattlesnakes are sidewinders (*Crotalus cerastes*), also called horned rattlesnakes for the unusual raised scales above their eyes. Found only in the Southwest U.S. and northwest Mexico, sidewinders are named for their explosive sideways locomotion, which propels them up to 18 mph—the fastest snakes in the world. The park is home to the Mojave Desert sidewinder and Colorado Desert sidewinder.

Mojave Desert Sidewinder

Rattlesnakes conjure fear in many visitors, but these relatively shy snakes are equally fearful of humans, whom they try to ward off by rattling their tail. The rattle consists of a series of dry, interlocking segments that, when shaken, produce an unforgettable sound. A new segment is added to the rattle each time the snake sheds its skin. The rattle's interlocking segments are made of keratin, the same material found in human hair and fingernails. If you hear a rattle, back away from the snake and give it plenty of space. Rattlesnakes prefer open, rocky habitat where hiding places are plentiful. While exploring the park, try not to put your hands or feet into dark rock crevices.

California Kingsnake

Rattlesnakes are considered some of the world's most highly evolved snakes. Although they have poor eyesight, they can detect prey in complete darkness using infrared sensors on either side of their head. They also boast exceptional smell, detecting scents through large nostrils and by flicking their long, forked-tongue to collect scent-bearing particles in the air. Rattlesnakes use these powerful senses to detect prey such as rodents and small birds while lying in wait. When a rattler strikes, it injects a paralyzing venom through sharp fangs. Once the victim is motionless, the rattler swallows it head-first. This allows bird wings or rodent limbs to fold inward, streamlining the swallowing process. The rattler then slowly digests the victim over several days. Rattlers, in turn, are preyed upon by owls and hawks, which pluck snakes from the ground and drop them repeatedly from the air to break their vertebrae.

Another notable rattlesnake predator is the California kingsnake (*Lampropeltis californiae*), which is immune to snake venom. Kingsnakes earned their name because they prey on other snakes. They strangle victims like boa constrictors, but unlike boas, which suffocate prey, kingsnakes subdue prey until it is completely exhausted, then swallow the hapless victim alive.

Red Racer

Gopher Snake

Gopher snakes (*Pituophis catenifer*) are sometimes confused with rattlesnakes due to their side-blotched coloration—a trait that helps non-venomous gopher snakes avoid predators. Growing up to seven feet long, gopher snakes are nocturnal hunters of small rodents, birds, and lizards. Like boas, gopher snakes constrict and suffocate prey. When threatened, gopher snakes produce a loud, prolonged hiss—a reaction unusual among snakes in the region. Two varieties of gopher snake call Joshua Tree home: the Sonoran gopher snake (*Pituophis catenifer affinis*) and Great Basin gopher snake (*Pituophis catenifer deserticola*).

Other non-venomous snakes in Joshua Tree include the red racer (*Coluber flagellum*), also known as the red coachwhip, and the rosy boa (*Lichanura orcutti*), the only boa constrictor in the park. The rosy boa, which lives in the Mojave and Sonoran Deserts, is one of just four boa species in the continental U.S. Growing up to 44 inches long, rosy boas have three colored stripes running the length of their body. The stripes are sometimes rosy-colored, giving the boa its common name, but they also come in a variety of colors ranging from orange to reddish brown.

Rosy Boa

Desert Iguana

Dipsosaurus dorsalis

These docile lizards, which grow up to two feet long, like it hot. They allow their internal body temperature to reach 115°F—the hottest voluntary temperature recorded in any vertebrate. This helps desert iguanas digest plant matter, which takes longer to break down than animal food. Desert iguanas hibernate from late October to March—nearly 40% of the year.

Mojave Fringe-toed Lizard

Uma scoparia

Exquisitely evolved to sandy environments, fringe-toed lizards sprint across sand dunes at speeds topping 22 mph. Large, fringed-toes function like snowshoes, offering superior traction in sand. Overlapping eyelids and nostril valves keep sand out of vital organs. In Joshua Tree, where dunes are scarce, Mojave fringe-toed lizards scamper around the wind-blown sands of washes and dry lake beds.

Horned Lizards

Blainville's Horned Lizard

With pointy horns and spiny body armor, horned lizards look like tiny, three-inch dinosaurs. Two species live in Joshua Tree: Blainville's horned lizard (*Phrynosoma blainvillii*) and desert horned lizard (*Phrynosoma platyrhinos*). Their mottled coloration is highly effective desert camouflage. Although relatively slow, their rugged armor deters predators by making them hard to swallow. When seriously threatened, horned lizards shoot blood from their eyes, which repels foxes and coyotes. Horned lizards are sit-and-wait predators that feed primarily on ants. They are often found dining at ant hills. Additional horned lizard prey includes grasshoppers, crickets, and beetles.

Desert Horned Lizard

Chuckwalla
Sauromalus ater

The largest lizard in Joshua Tree—and the second-largest lizard in North America after Gila monsters—chuckwallas measure up to 20 inches long and weigh up to two pounds. They have round bellies, thick tails, and loose folds of skin around the neck and shoulders. Chuckwallas range from southern Utah to Mexico's Baja Peninsula. After a cold night, they bask in the morning sun until their internal body temperature reaches 100°F, at which point they search for food. Chuckwallas are California's only strict vegetarian lizard, browsing on flowers, leaves, buds, and fruit. When threatened or frightened, chuckwallas retreat to rocky crevices, wedging themselves in place by inflating their lungs up to three times normal breathing capacity. This unusual defense mechanism deters all but the most dogged predators. Indigenous tribes consider chuckwalla meat a delicacy, and hunters punctured inflated lizards with sharp sticks to remove them from their hiding places. Chuckwallas mate in spring, and females lay clutches of five to ten eggs in summer. Dominant males, called tyrants, defend their territory through physical displays such as push-ups, head-bobbing, and mouth gaping. Males with the largest tails are generally the most dominant and do the most mating.

Desert Night Lizard
Xantusia vigilis

Weighing less than two grams, desert night lizards are North America's smallest reptile and the lizard most closely associated with Joshua trees. Desert night lizards thrive under fallen Joshua tree branches, happily devouring termites that feed on the cellulose. The lizards, in turn, are hunted by desert night snakes (*Hypsiglena chlorophaea*). Like many lizards, desert night lizards have detachable tails to thwart predators. After detaching, the tail wriggles vigorously, distracting the predator while the lizard escapes.

Red-Spotted Toad

Anaxyrus punctatu

This unusual toad, found only in the U.S. Southwest and northwestern Mexico, is a true desert survivor. Although common throughout Joshua Tree, it spends much of its life underground waiting for seasonal rains. Following a rainstorm, red-spotted toads emerge from their hiding places. After quickly rehydrating, they mate and lay eggs in temporary pools of water. At that point it's a race against evaporation. Eggs hatch in just three days, and tadpoles transform into toads in six to eight weeks. Adult red-spotted toads, which are easily identified by bright red wart-like glands, grow up to three inches long. Though slow and clumsy, toads deter predators by secreting toxic fluids from their glands.

California Tree Frog

Pseudacris cadaverina

The duck-like vocalizations of these two-inch tree frogs echo through rocky canyons at night. In Joshua Tree, California tree frogs cluster near permanent water sources on the northern edge of the park. They likely arrived during the Ice Age, when today's desert was lush and green, then became an isolated population as temperatures dried out. Today Joshua Tree marks the eastern limit of their range, which stretches from San Luis Obispo to Baja, Mexico.

Desert Banded Gecko

Coleonyx variegatus

Growing up to six inches long, this desert gecko emerges at night when other lizards are resting. Desert banded geckos can be active with a body temperature 18°F cooler than other lizards, allowing them to forage at night. Their diet includes insects, spiders, and newborn scorpions. When food is scarce, desert banded geckos can survive up to nine months off water and fat stored in the tail. Geckos are unique among lizards for their squeaky vocalizations.

Tarantula
Aphonopelma iodium

Tarantulas, the world's largest spiders, measure up to eight inches long in Joshua Tree. Thousands of sensitive hairs help them detect the motion of nearby prey. Tarantulas eat anything they can chase down, including insects, lizards, and even small mammals. After injecting prey with paralyzing venom, tarantulas secrete a digestive enzyme that liquefies the victim's organs. Tarantulas then suck the liquefied organs out with straw-like mouths. (Fortunately, tarantula bites are harmless to humans.) Tarantulas are most active during fall mating season, when males wander the park in search of female burrows.

Tarantula Hawk
Pepsis formosa

This large wasp, which grows up to two inches long, is a tarantula's worst nightmare. After locating a tarantula, a female tarantula hawk paralyzes it with venom, then drags it back to her burrow. After laying eggs on the tarantulas body, she seals the burrow—effectively burying the spider alive. When larvae hatch, they feast on the still-living tarantula. Larvae eat non-essential body parts first, keeping the spider alive as long as possible to maximize freshness.

Giant Hairy Scorpion
Hadrurus arizonensis

Growing over five inches long, giant hairy scorpions are the largest scorpions in the U.S. Although common in Joshua Tree, they are nocturnal and rarely seen. Scorpions feed on insects, tarantulas, small lizards, and snakes. Brown hairs, which cover the scorpion's body and inspire its common name, detect prey by sensing tiny vibrations on the ground. The famous stinger, located at the tip of the abdomen, is thrust over the head to inject venom when prey cannot be subdued with pincers alone. Although the giant hairy scorpion's sting is painful to humans, its effect is about the same as a honeybee.

Oasis of Mara

HISTORY

IN THE DEPTHS of the Ice Age, Joshua Tree was a very different place. As massive glaciers advanced over much of North America, they pushed the Jet Stream south, transforming Southern California into lush, green environment filled with rivers and lakes. In Joshua Tree National Park, mammoths, mastodons, and camels wandered grassy plains, and a river flowed through Pinto Basin.

When the Pleistocene ended 11,700 years ago, global temperatures were on the rise. Glaciers melted, the Jet Stream drifted north, and the climate of Southern California dried out. As early as 8,000 years ago, humans took up residence in Pinto Basin. Very little is known about these ancient people, who are called the Pinto Culture. The only evidence of their existence comes from stone tools and spear points discovered by archaeologists. The abundance of spear points suggests the Pinto Culture depended on large game. Hunters attached stone points to wooden spears, and used spear throwers (atlatls) to hurl weapons at animals. The Pinto Culture may have occupied Pinto Basin for as long as 4,000 years, but eventually they abandoned the area. What triggered their exodus remains a mystery. By the time they left, Pinto Basin's river had dried up and the Ice Age megafauna were long gone.

Several thousand years later, the Serrano and Cahuilla arrived in the park. Both tribes visited on a seasonal basis, taking advantage of resources when they were abundant. The Serrano spent winters in the northern half of Joshua Tree and summers in the cool pine forests of the San Bernardino Mountains. The Cahuilla visited the southern half of the park, which marked the northern limit of their range. Both tribes belong to the Uto-Aztecan language family. They share similar cultures, and they have long been linked through intermarriage and trade. Despite their close ties and close proximity, however, the Serrano and Cahuilla have always remained two distinct tribes.

There are only so many ways to survive in the desert, however, so in terms of day-to-day activities the Serrano and Cahuilla were virtually identical. The same was true

Pinto Projectile Point

of most desert tribes in Southern California, where the harsh environment forced people to adapt in remarkably similar ways. Limited resources kept population densities low, with villages generally consisting of 25 to 100 people. This was a stark contrast to tribes on the coast where abundant resources supported villages of 1,000 people or more.

Desert tribes hunted large and small game, but up to three-quarters of their diet consisted of plants. Acorns, mesquite beans, and pine nuts were the most important foods, but they ate over 100 plant varieties. Because different plants have different growing seasons, desert tribes were highly mobile, moving from one harvesting site to another throughout the year.

Hunters harvested large animals such as deer and bighorn sheep, but they generally preferred smaller prey such as jackrabbits and rodents, which were more plentiful, less dangerous, and easier to hunt. Hunting weapons included bows, arrows, and throwing sticks similar to boomerangs that broke an animal's legs. Hunters extracted rodents hiding in rock crevices or burrows with long, forked sticks that were twisted into the animal's fur. Desert tribes were not particularly picky eaters, however, and their diet also included snakes, lizards, and insect larvae. Crickets were roasted as a condiment for acorn mush. Although the Serrano and Cahuilla ate just about anything that moved, they also kept dogs, birds, and reptiles as pets.

In winter, men and women wore animal skin clothing. In summer, they wore few clothes at all. Women were highly skilled weavers, and they spent much of their time weaving plant fibers from yuccas and desert fan palms into baskets, hats, sandals, netting, and rope. A woman's social prestige was often based on her weaving ability. Pottery was another important skill, and desert tribes stored food and water in earthen vessels called ollas.

Serrano & Cahuilla pottery & basketry

Oasis of Mara

The Serrano and Cahuilla constructed thatched huts from palm fronds. Each family lived in a circular house with a central fire pit, but most aspects of daily life happened outside. During the day, villagers sat in the shade of a ramada, a thatched canopy supported by four poles. Villages also had communal structures such as storage buildings, sweat houses, and large ceremonial rooms. The largest village in Joshua Tree was located at the Oasis of Mara, where a cluster of desert fan palms provided abundant resources for the Serrano, supporting dozens of people at its peak.

Each village had a leader, but daily life revolved around the family. Family members depended on one another for survival, and their bonds lay at the heart of Serrano and Cahuilla society. The importance of family is reflected in vocabulary—the Cahuilla have over 60 words describing relatives and relationships.

Both the Serrano and Cahuilla split themselves into two distinct groups called *moieties*, based on male family lineage. The two moieties—*Tukum* ("Wildcats") and *Wahilyam* ("Coyotes")—serve mostly as marriage guides. A Wildcat can marry a Coyote, for example, but not another Wildcat. Likewise, a Coyote can marry a Wildcat, but not another Coyote. These rules encourage a healthy and diverse gene pool. They also encourage young people to seek partners outside their village, strengthening overall alliances within the tribe.

EUROPEAN COLONIZATION

For centuries the Serrano and Cahuilla led challenging but comfortable lives. The desert's resources were limited, but both tribes made the most of them, and they generally enjoyed peaceful relationships with neighboring tribes. The combined population of the Serrano and Cahuilla probably never exceeded more than 3,000 people, but they made unique contributions to California's rich native culture.

Prior to European colonization, California was home to roughly 100,000 indigenous people spread among 60 or so tribes. In 1542, two decades after Spain conquered the Aztecs, Juan Rodriguez Cabrillo sailed north from Mexico to explore California's coast. Cabrillo recorded favorable impressions of the land, but Spain saw little economic opportunity in the arid backwater. There were no empires to conquer, no cities filled with gold, and California lay half a world away from major centers of trade. For the next two centuries, California served mostly as a backdrop for smugglers sailing between Mexico and Asia.

Then, in the mid-1700s, Russian fur trappers began venturing down North America's Pacific Coast. Madrid immediately grew alarmed. To "guard the dominions from all invasion and insult," Spain ordered the construction of 21 missions along the California coast. In 1771, Mission San Gabriel Archangel opened in present-day Los Angeles. Although European goods drifted east along native trade routes, desert tribes had virtually no contact with the Spanish, who largely avoided the desert.

It wasn't until 1775 that Franciscan missionary Francisco Garcés undertook the first meaningful exploration of California's deserts. During a nearly year-long, 2,000-mile trek, Garcés went native. He adopted the clothes and eating habits of local tribes, and he dutifully chronicled his observations. Among other things, Garcés noted a thriving slave trade operated by the Mohave tribe along the Colorado River.

Spanish authorities, meanwhile, were focused on problems along the coast. Mission uprisings had grown increasingly common, and Mission Indians who escaped often fled inland to California's remote deserts and mountains. While there, they recruited local tribes to raid Mission livestock. To bring these remote tribes under control, the Spanish built an interior chain of outposts called *asistencias* that ran parallel to Missions on the coast.

In 1819, Mission San Gabriel built an asistencia in Redlands, less than 40 miles from present-day Joshua Tree National Park. The Serrano and Cahuilla living near Redlands were soon under Spanish control, but more distant villages, including those in Joshua Tree, were relatively protected by the rugged Little San Bernardino Mountains.

Spanish Mission

Just two years after the asistencia in Redlands was established, the Mexican Revolution ended Spanish control of California. Within a few years, the Mission system dissolved. Mission life had been difficult for native tribes, but the transition away from Mission life proved just as taxing. Many former Mission Indians were hired as cheap labor by powerful Mexican ranchers who controlled the region. The ranchers generally stayed clear of the deserts, however, which meant tribes living there enjoyed traditional lifestyles.

A few decades later, Anglo explorers from the east arrived in California. Most were destined for the coast, but a few passed through Serrano and Cahuilla territory along the way. Fur trapper Jedediah Smith crossed the Mojave Desert north of Joshua Tree in 1826, and Kit Carson followed in his footsteps a few years later. When explorer John Fremont passed through the Mojave in 1844, he noted: "From all that I heard and saw I should say that humanity here appears in its lowest form and in its most elemental state." He also described Joshua trees as "the most repulsive tree in the vegetable kingdom."

Fremont's gruff description was typical of white attitudes towards deserts and desert inhabitants. In the days before air conditioning and automobiles, deserts were considered deadly, hostile terrain. The first Spanish expedition into the desert was only organized after a group of military deserters fled there hoping they wouldn't be followed. Only a handful of expeditions were organized after that. By the time the United States gained control of California in 1848, its deserts were among the most remote and unexplored regions in the country. But all that was about to change.

THE CALIFORNIA GOLD RUSH

On January 24, 1848, nine days before Mexico officially handed over California to the United States, James Marshall discovered gold in the foothills of the Sierra Nevada Mountains. Both countries were unaware of the discovery when the papers were signed, but within months the biggest gold rush in the history of the world was on. Prior to 1848, only a few thousand white settlers lived in California. In 1849 alone, over 80,000 people flooded the golden state. A decade later California's population neared 400,000.

California was booming, but the influx was almost entirely concentrated in the northern half of the state. In 1860, over a decade after the Gold Rush kicked off, Los Angeles remained a small cattle ranching town with barely 2,000 residents. The deserts to the east were almost completely untouched. In 1853, a scout for the U.S. Railroad Survey wrote of the region surrounding Joshua Tree: "Nothing is known of this country. I have never heard of a white man who had penetrated it."

Amazing Acorns

Of all the world's early human cultures, only in North America did complex inland societies evolve in the absence of agriculture. All other complex societies, from the Egyptians to the Aztecs, fueled their development on irrigated crops, which are highly nutritious and capable of mass production. But the indigenous tribes north of Mexico were not only able to survive without large-scale farming, they advanced to the point of developing complex, multi-tiered societies run by ruling elites and distinguished by ritual specialists and skilled craftsmen. Anthropologists had once assumed agriculture was essential for such a feat. The indigenous people of North America proved them wrong.

What made their situation different was North America's staggering abundance of natural resources. Even away from the seafood-rich coasts, the continent's unique topography lent itself to a wilderness flush with wild game and edible plants. Although both were eaten, plants were the most important food source. And from the deserts of California to the forests of New England, the most important plants were oak trees and the acorns they provided.

In other parts of the world, nuts are covered in shells so thick you need a hammer to open them (think macadamias and brazils). But North American varieties are different. Here, nuts like acorns are thin-shelled and easy to open. They are also highly nutritious and can be harvested in enormous quantities. At large oak groves, a single adult can collect several tons of acorns over the course of a two-week harvest. Acorns can also be stored for up to a year without spoiling because of the presence of a natural preservative called tannin. Tannin increases the acorn's shelf-life, but it also makes them bitter and unpalatable. It's the same chemical used to tan leather. To make acorns edible, native women ground them into an oily meal that was filtered repeatedly with water to leach out tannins. The resulting flour was cooked into a gruel-like soup or tortilla-style flatbread.

The autumn acorn harvest was so important among Southern California tribes that elaborate rituals and ceremonies developed around it. When acorns ripened, village leaders proclaimed a three-day festival of feasting, singing, and dancing to celebrate the harvest.

Since the arrival of Spanish colonists, California's deserts acted as a natural barrier between tribes living there and white settlers on the coast. During the first decade of the Gold Rush, native populations were decimated across much of California. But tribes in the remote deserts remained relatively unaffected. Then, in 1863, the natural barrier was shattered when smallpox swept through Los Angeles and headed east along native trade routes. Within weeks, many Serrano and Cahuilla fell ill.

For centuries desert shaman treated sick people by sending them into sweat houses. After entering an enclosed shack heated by fire, the sick person sweated profusely for hours—a treatment believed to cleanse the body and promote health. But sweat houses were disastrous when applied to smallpox. Gathering in sweat houses increased rates of transmission, which accelerated spread across the desert. Native populations plummeted. Entire villages were abandoned. Within months, the social and political structures that governed desert tribes for centuries began to fall apart.

Among those who abandoned their village were the Serrano at the Oasis of Mara. When survivors returned a few years later, they found a group of Chemeheuvi living among the palms. The Chemeheuvi were the Serrano's eastern neighbors, but a series of wars with the more powerful Mohave tribe along the Colorado River had forced the Chemeheuvi west.

Both tribes had fallen on hard times, and they agreed to share resources at the oasis. Sadly, the Chemeheuvi and Serrano were facing the end of their traditional lifestyle, which had defined their cultures for centuries. As more white settlers arrived in California, native populations continued to decline. By the late 1800s, over 75 percent of California's native population had perished due to disease and warfare. A government report issued towards the end of the century summed up the situation in one sentence: "Never before in history has a people been swept away with such terrible swiftness."

Smallpox was among the deadliest killers the world has ever known. The virus killed much of North America's indigenous population, and in the 18th century alone it killed an estimated 60 million people in Europe. In the 20th century, smallpox killed up to 500 million people worldwide. In 1980, after a multi-decade vaccination campaign, the World Health Organization certified the worldwide eradication of smallpox. It remains the only human virus ever eradicated.

GOLD MINERS IN JOSHUA TREE

Smallpox critically weakened tribes living at the Oasis of Mara, but the final blow came from the rapid development of Southern California in the late 1800s. By the 1850s, San Bernardino ranchers were driving cattle into the Mojave Desert. Before long they had ventured into the protected valleys and grasslands in the northern half of present-day Joshua Tree National Park.

Ranching in the desert required about 17 acres per adult animal. But ranchers were often on the go, moving seasonally in search of adequate food and water. As one early rancher put it, "In those days, if you were a cowpuncher, you had a pair of chaps, a horse and a pack horse, a bedroll, salt, staples, a six-shooter, and a big chew of tobacco." Ranchers were the first whites to become familiar with the area, and they built a network of primitive access roads. Many roads were simply improved native trails, but their impact on the region was dramatic.

By the mid-1850s, as Northern California's gold fields started to dwindle, thousands of prospectors fanned out across the state in search of the next big strike. A handful wandered along the roads that led to Joshua Tree, and in 1863 they discovered gold near the Oasis of Mara. Tribes living at the oasis suddenly found themselves sharing its resources with white prospectors. In the beginning, the prospectors only stayed briefly. Then, in 1879, the region received its first permanent white settler: Bill McHaney. Just 20 years old, McHaney would stay in the area until his death nearly 60 years later. Naturally friendly, McHaney got along so well with local tribes that they showed him the locations of nearby trails, water holes, and gold deposits.

But the region's defining moment came in 1883, when a prospector named Lew Curtis wandered into the foothills 15 miles east of the Oasis of Mara. Curtis discovered deposits so rich the ground literally glittered with gold. When the news leaked out, hundreds of prospectors flocked to the area, and a boomtown named Dale rose up nearby.

At its rough and tumble peak, Dale was home to over 1,000 people—almost one-tenth the size of Los Angeles at the time. Most of Dale's citizens lived in portable tents. When a new strike was discovered, the town packed up and moved on. In its early years, Dale's location shifted several times. When the town finally settled down, it boasted a general store, post office, blacksmith, and saloon. A small shack on a hill overlooking Dale constituted the red light district, jokingly referred to as the "Mayor's Residence."

Dale's initial residents collected placer gold—small bits of gold eroded from rich veins. Often this gold was simply scattered along the ground. When the placer gold was gone, prospectors turned their attention to the rich veins, which were buried deep underground in lode deposits. Lode mining was expensive and complicated, however, and most prospectors lacked the money and expertise it required. At this point well-capitalized mining companies arrived in Dale. Before long, many of the town's citizens had become salaried employees.

After working all day in the mines, Dale's residents returned in the early evening to gamble and drink into the night. There were only a handful of buildings in town, so most activities took place outside at tables illuminated by kerosene lanterns. Dale's saloon was reserved for the town's most important citizens, a group that included mine owners, engineers, assayers, and shift foremen. The saloon boasted a primitive air-conditioning system that consisted of a wall of canvas kept constantly wet. As water on the canvas evaporated, it cooled the interior of the saloon.

But creature comforts were few and far between, especially for the working class. Miners worked long hours, often in triple-digit heat, and prospectors not employed by mining companies often came home empty-handed. Dale's water was pumped from a well north of town, and it arrived in Dale tinted brown with minerals and salts. These living conditions were more than most men could bear. After a few years, Dale's population dwindled. A few grizzled prospectors kept searching for gold, and occasionally they found it. By the turn of the century, a handful of mines had been discovered that rivaled those at Dale, most notably Lost Horse Mine and Desert Queen Mine. For a few rough and tumble decades, gold mining flourished in the region.

Gold Mining

IN THE

Desert

Millions of years ago, gold-bearing magma welled up below Joshua Tree and seeped into cracks in the bedrock. After cooling and hardening, the magma formed long quartz veins speckled with gold particles. Over time, erosion exposed the quartz veins, and small grains of placer gold spread across the landscape. *Placer* is Spanish for "pleasure"—a reference to the relative ease of gathering this form of gold. When prospectors first arrived in Joshua Tree in the late 1800s, they collected small grains of placer gold by dry washing. This involved gathering gold-rich soil in a pan and repeatedly tossing it in the air, letting the wind blow away the lighter soil particles and leaving the heavier gold particles behind. Dry washing was time consuming, but it was easy and inexpensive. When the placer gold was gone, prospectors turned to lode deposits found in underground quartz veins. They mined huge quantities of quartz ore, which was then processed by stamp mills to separate gold particles from the rest of the rock. Miners were lucky to extract ¼ ounce of gold from one ton of crushed ore.

Stamp Mill

1 Small chunks of crushed ore are placed in a mesh chamber.

2 A heavy iron cylinder, the "stamp," moves up and down, pulverizing the ore into a fine powder.

3 Water flushes out the powder, spreading a mushy pulp over the amalgam board.

4 Gold particles cling to mercury on the amalgam board. Other particles wash away. The gold and mercury mixture is then scraped off and heated. The mercury vaporizes, leaving gold behind.

Willie Boy

THE WILLIE BOY MANHUNT

In the late 1800s, the dirt roads leading white ranchers and prospectors into the Joshua Tree region were also leading natives out. Many Serrano and Chemehuevi accepted seasonal employment at ranches. For a few months each year, native families lived and worked at ranches, collecting a steady paycheck. They were adapting to the modern world, but they were also competing with poor whites. It wasn't long before racial tensions flared. Unsolved crimes were frequently blamed on innocent natives, some of whom were hunted down in brutal raids. Towards the end of the century, one government employee concluded that "Race prejudice is too strong in Southern California to secure a fair administration of justice."

Discrimination was a fact of life in the region, but native people were also facing problems within their own tribes. Poverty, alcoholism, and a new generation of young people fascinated by white culture were taking a toll on traditional lifestyles. As tribal elders passed away, there were fewer young people left to replace them. Those that could were sometimes reluctant to do so. This intergenerational tension came to a breaking point when two young people living at the Oasis of Mara fell in love.

In 1909, a 27-year-old Chemeheuvi named Willie Boy became romantically involved with Carlota Boniface, the 16-year-old daughter of Old Mike Boniface, one of the leading elders of the Chemeheuvi tribe. When Willie Boy approached Old Mike for permission to marry, he was vehemently denied. Willie Boy and Carlota belonged to the same moiety, and traditional Chemeheuvi culture forbid the couple from marrying. Old Mike was furious that Willie Boy would even consider the prospect.

Shortly after Old Mike's rejection, Willie Boy and Carlota ran away into the desert together. Within a few hours, Old Mike tracked them down and confronted Willie Boy at gunpoint. The young lovers were brought back to the village and physically separated.

A few months later, Willie Boy shot Old Mike Boniface at point blank range. He then fled into the desert with Carlota at his side. The nearby town of Banning organized a white posse to capture the pair, but by the time they left Willie Boy and Carlota had a six-hour head start.

The posse returned to Banning three days later with the body of Carlota Boniface. As a horrified crowd gathered, the posse explained that she had been shot by Willie Boy when she slowed his escape. According to the posse, Willie Boy left her for dead and continued running on his own.

Carlota's murder marked a pivotal turning point in the Willie Boy saga. Prior to her death, many whites brushed off Old Mike's murder as an Indian dispute. There was even something romantic and thrilling about two young lovers running away together. Carlota's murder changed all that. Suddenly, Willie Boy was no longer a misguided lover but a cold-blooded killer, motivated by raw savagery. For decades white settlers had fought to civilize the West. Willie Boy's actions represented an affront to their accomplishments. On a much darker level, it also confirmed the suspicions of many white settlers regarding the true nature of Indian behavior.

Within 24 hours of the posse's return, a second posse was dispatched. Reward posters were printed, and local newspapers fueled interest in the manhunt. Their coverage quickly degenerated into tabloid fiction playing up popular Western stereotypes. Willie Boy was a "red-skinned lady killer" as "fickle as he was gallant in affairs of the heart." When one of the posse members claimed, with no evidence, that an empty bottle of whiskey was found in Willie Boy's bedroom, a paper reported that Willie Boy consumed "a suitcase full of whiskey" before shooting Mike Boniface. Before long half a dozen other gratuitous killings were added to his record.

Over the next several days, Willie Boy used a combination of speed and cunning to elude the posse. He headed east toward Nevada before cutting back to the San Bernardino Mountains, just west of Joshua Tree. As the posse approached the mountains, Willie Boy's tracks included a narrow line in the sand. He was dragging his rifle. They were finally wearing him down.

Willie Boy's tracks led to Ruby Mountain, located on the western fringe of the San Bernardino Mountains. As the posse approached the mountain, Willie Boy fired from above. One man was seriously wounded. The posse fired back and sought cover. Words and shots were exchanged throughout the day, but the wounded man's condition forced the posse to withdraw. Just before they left, a final shot echoed from the mountain. No bullet landed anywhere near the men.

—— DESERT RUNNERS ——

Willie Boy's physical accomplishments during the manhunt cannot be overstated. For over a full week, traveling on foot, he eluded five men chasing him on horseback. He covered nearly 600 miles of desert terrain, sometimes averaging 50 miles *a day*. At times, the posse's horses grew so tired the men had to dismount and continue on foot. Some scholars have suggested that Willie Boy was genetically predisposed to excel at running. For hundreds of years, a cult of runners existed within the Chemeheuvi tribe that served as desert messengers, covering vast stretches of rugged terrain with astonishing speed. Willie Boy was a gifted baseball player known for his athleticism. It's possible his ancestors belonged to the Chemeheuvi running cult.

TELL THEM WILLIE BOY IS HERE

Exactly 60 years after the Willie Boy manhunt, Universal Pictures released *Tell Them Willie Boy Is Here*, a film loosely based on the actual events. It starred Robert Redford as a fictional sheriff named Cooper, Robert Blake (in redface) as Willie Boy, and Katherine Ross as Willie Boy's lover. Abraham Polonski wrote and directed *Tell Them Willie Boy Is Here*, which marked his directorial return after being blacklisted for communist activities. Polonski presented a largely sympathetic story in which Willie Boy is a victim of conflicting white and native cultures.

Around the time of the film's release, some Hollywood luminaries were championing a "new Indian movie" in which traditional western stereotypes were cast aside. In 1973, Marlon Brando protested Hollywood's depiction of Indians by sending a woman in buckskin clothes to the Oscars to decline his Best Actor award for *The Godfather*. The woman, Sacheen Littlefeet, accepted Brando's award and gave a politically charged speech expressing her views on "the treatment of Indians today by the film industry." Moments later, when Clint Eastwood took the stage to announce Best Picture, he prefaced his remarks by saying, "I hope I don't have to present this award to all the cowboys shot in John Ford Westerns."

Jim & Matilda Pine

Within hours news of the shootout reached Banning, and newspapers went to press with heavily fictionalized accounts. While Banning newspapers dished out sensationalized gossip, the town of Riverside, located near Banning, prepared for the arrival of President William Howard Taft. Taft was in the middle of a cross-country speaking tour, and an entourage of East Coast reporters followed along. When the reporters learned of the Willie Boy manhunt, they jumped on the story. New York editorial pages soon fretted that Willie Boy represented a credible threat to the President's life. Before long, newspapers across the country were covering the manhunt.

As Willie Boy rumors swirled around the nation, a third posse approached Ruby Mountain. As they neared the spot where Willie Boy was last seen, they found his bloated, sunburned body lying on the ground. A rifle lay by his side. At the end of the last shootout, Willie Boy had removed his shoe, pointed his rifle at his chest, and pulled the trigger with his big toe.

The gruesome discovery brought the Willie Boy manhunt to a close. In the aftermath, however, most Serrano and Chemehuevi living at the Oasis of Mara decided to leave the village for good. Some believed it was now haunted by evil spirits. Others were simply fed up with the challenge of living there. For decades tribes at the Oasis of Mara had been involved in a bitter land dispute with Southern Pacific Railroad. The bad press generated by the Willie Boy manhunt tipped the scales in the railroad's favor. Only two people, an elderly couple named Jim and Matilda Pine, refused to leave the village, insisting on spending their final days near the graves of their children. By 1912, however, even the Pines were gone.

Was Willie Boy Innocent?

Decades after the Willie Boy manhunt, some scholars concluded the posse's story was a lie. They believed it was a posse member, not Willie Boy, who shot Carlota. According to this theory, when Carlota could no longer keep up with Willie Boy, he tried to hide her and lead the posse away on his own. When the posse approached Carlota's hiding spot, they saw a figure moving in the distance and fired. Only when they drew near did they realized they had shot Carlota. The murder of the 16-year-old girl they were trying to rescue was a disaster. To cover up the situation, the men pinned the murder on Willie Boy. Scholars point out that when Carlota's body was "discovered," it was surrounded by most of Willie Boy's supplies, including a canteen of water. Why Willie Boy would abandon critical supplies and murder the girl he loved is indeed a mystery.

THE LEGENDARY BILL KEYS

The departure of native tribes from the Oasis of Mara marked a notable shift in the region. For the next several decades local culture would be defined entirely by white miners, cattlemen, and homesteaders. The most famous member of this group was a man named Bill Keys, who arrived in 1910 and spent most of his life in present-day Joshua Tree National Park.

Keys came to Twentynine Palms at the age of 30, having spent much of his youth wandering the Southwest. He became superintendent of the once profitable Desert Queen Mine, but shortly after his arrival the mining company he worked for went bankrupt. As compensation for back wages, Keys was offered the deed to the mine, which he gladly accepted. He then homesteaded 160 acres and built himself a nearby ranch.

Several years later, on a rare trip to Los Angeles, Keys wandered into a department store and met a young saleswoman named Frances May Lawton. In 1918, the couple were married. Frances moved in with Bill at his remote ranch, and they started a family. Frances gave birth to seven children, three of whom died while still young. The surviving Keys children grew up in frontier conditions. There was no plumbing, no electricity, and the nearest town was a two-day wagon ride away. Physically separated from much of the outside world, the family survived almost entirely on local resources.

The biggest challenge in the desert was securing a steady supply of water. Keys overcame this by expanding nearby Barker Dam to create a small reservoir. He stocked the reservoir with fish and installed pipes that irrigated an orchard and garden at his ranch. The family swam in the reservoir in summer and ice skated on it in winter.

Bill's days were filled with hard physical labor. When he wasn't mining or ranching, he tended to the physical upkeep of his property. Frances spent her time gardening, cooking, and tending to animals on the ranch. The children were responsible for a wide variety of chores. In their free time the Keys children amused themselves mostly with their imaginations. As one of them later recalled, "Our toys were usually pieces of iron or wood."

Bill Keys was a born scavenger, a trait that served him well in the desert. Basic goods were always in short supply, and Keys was always on the lookout for scraps. Over the course of his life, Keys claimed 35 local mine and mill sites, many of which were abandoned. Often he was less interested in the mine or the mill than the machinery and spare parts that came with them. His collection of odds and ends was legendary. Whenever local settlers needed tools or spare parts, they always turned to Keys, who accepted cash but preferred trading for additional spare parts.

Bill Keys

Worth Bagley Tombstone

GUNFIGHT IN JOSHUA TREE

Bill Keys got along well with most of his neighbors, but local tensions sometimes flared. Most disputes were triggered by the desert's limited resources, and most were settled far from the eyes of the law. In 1929, Keys shot and wounded a local cowboy over a contested water well. Following the incident, Keys developed a mixed reputation. Although many knew him as a fair and honest man, those who quarreled with him understood his good nature had its breaking point.

About a decade after the incident at the well, Keys became involved in another dispute. This one was with a retired Los Angeles Sheriff named Worth Bagley, who supposedly moved to the region for health reasons. In reality, Bagley had been discharged from the police force due to questionable sanity and repeated abuses of power. Following his arrival in Joshua Tree, he developed a reputation as a loose cannon. He was constantly armed and often angry. And much of his anger was directed at his closest neighbor: Bill Keys.

Among other things, Bagley claimed that Keys' "vicious" cattle were constantly bothering him. When Keys found some of his cattle shot, he blamed the killings on Bagley. Bagley responded by lashing out at Keys. "You've accused me of shooting your cattle," Bagley told Keys. "Don't never accuse me of that again or the next time I shoot, it won't be cattle."

But the greatest point of contention involved a formerly public road that passed over part of Bagley's property. Keys had used the road for years, but Bagley told him, in no uncertain terms, that he was no longer welcome on it. Keys ignored Bagley, and the men grew so angry with one another that they stopped talking entirely. Bagley then upped the ante by sprinkling the contested road with broken glass and blocking it with fallen Joshua trees.

On May 11, 1943, as Keys drove along the public section of Bagley's road, he encountered a hand-drawn sign. "Keys," the sign read, "this is my last warning. Stay off my property." Keys looked up and saw Bagley approaching in the distance with a revolver. Keys grabbed his rifle but waited for Bagley to fire the first shot. Bagley fired and missed. Keys fired three shots in response, and Bagley's body fell to the ground.

Later that day Keys drove to Twentynine Palms to notify the authorities that he had shot and killed Worth Bagley in self-defense. Seven weeks later, Keys was brought to trial. The prosecution argued that Keys had deliberately murdered Bagley, then tampered with the evidence. A doctor testified that Bagley had been shot while running away, thus invalidating Keys' claim of self-defense. At the end of the trial, Keys was convicted of manslaughter and sentenced to 10 years in San Quentin Prison. He was 64 years old.

Following Keys' conviction, his wife Frances devoted herself to obtaining a pardon for her husband. But the family's resources were limited, and Frances accomplished little on her own. In desperation she wrote to one of Bill's old friends, a Ventura lawyer named Erle Stanley Gardner.

Keys had met Gardner in the late 1920s when Gardner came to Joshua Tree to camp. Years later, Gardner wrote a series of legal thrillers based on a fictional character named Perry Mason. When the books became best-sellers, Gardner used his celebrity to start a magazine column called "The Court of Last Resort." The column featured case histories of potentially innocent men who might have been wrongly convicted. After Gardner presented the evidence, readers decided whether the case should be handed over to a panel of experts for further investigation. When Gardner received Frances' letter, he immediately agreed to feature Keys's case.

By the time Gardner's article appeared, Keys had already spent four years in San Quentin Prison. Following the article's publication, readers flooded Gardner with letters demanding that Keys' case be reviewed. A team of volunteer experts reexamined the evidence and concluded that Keys had been wrongly convicted. After presenting their findings to the state, Keys was granted a full pardon.

Five and a half years after Bill Keys entered prison, he walked out a free and vindicated man. He later referred to his time in prison as his "education" because he spent his days reading, catching up on current affairs, and learning how to play guitar. Keys lived and worked at his ranch for the rest of his life, becoming something of a local celebrity in his later years. His grizzled looks, checkered past, and friendly disposition gave him the aura of a Grandpa of the Old West. When Walt Disney Studios came to Joshua Tree in the 1960s to film *The Wild Burro of the West*, the director was so taken with Keys' that he offered him a walk-on role as a grizzled old prospector.

In 1963, Frances Keys passed away. Bill Keys buried her at Desert Queen Ranch, and six years later he was laid to rest beside her. The couple had spent the better part of their lives in Joshua Tree, developing a bond with the environment that will probably never be surpassed by another white couple. In this stark and challenging landscape Bill Keys carved out his own unique life, guided by nothing more than his principles and rugged sense of self.

As Bill's son Willis later put it: "Dad was friendly and liked to get along with people, but had a lot of poor experiences with some people, and he wouldn't let anyone run over him. He said, 'Well, if the law won't uphold me, I'll uphold myself.' And he did. He liked nature, and anybody that liked nature, he liked them. He liked the open country, and he liked fairness."

Desert Queen Ranch

Minerva Hoyt

MINERVA HOYT'S MONUMENT

Over the course of his life, Bill Keys watched the Joshua Tree region change dramatically. In 1910, when he first arrived, the desert was a wild and remote place. Twentynine Palms was little more than a cluster of primitive shacks, and permanent settlers were few and far between. The most advanced form of transportation was the mule-drawn wagon train, and the closest town, Banning, was a two-day wagon ride away.

People drawn to this kind of environment were usually gold miners, cattle ranchers, or tuberculosis victims hoping the dry air would improve their health. As the century progressed, however, this motley demographic began to change. Thanks in large part to air conditioning, the desert became the realm of ordinary, everyday people. By the end of the century, some parts of the desert were among the fastest growing regions in California, with golf courses and strip malls claiming vast stretches of unlikely terrain.

The civilization—and later, suburbanization—of the desert traces its roots to a confluence of events in the early 1900s. When the century began, the population of Southern California was exploding. Railroads, which initially serviced only Northern California, now provided Southern California with a direct link to Eastern cities. Thousands of Easterners moved to Los Angeles in search of warm weather and cheap real estate. When the Panama Canal opened in 1914, Los Angeles became the busiest harbor on the West Coast. The local economy boomed. The population of Los Angeles reached 1 million people in 1920, then doubled over the next decade.

As Los Angeles grew, city sprawl edged closer to the desert. At the same time the city's residents were unleashed by the automobile, which provided a safe, dependable way to explore the desert. Day trips became common, and newspapers published motorlogues filled with maps and detailed information.

The desert's sudden popularity caused a number of problems. In the 1920s, Los Angeles gardeners became obsessed with exotic desert plants, and enterprising landscapers uprooted them by the truckload. Their impact was swift and dramatic. A popular destination called Devil's Garden, located just south of Joshua Tree, was once filled with thousands of yucca and cacti. By 1930, it had been stripped bare. Even today, plant life at Devil's Garden has yet to fully recover.

Some motorists set Joshua Trees on fire at night, supposedly as a guide for other travelers. In 1930, the tallest known Joshua tree, which towered over 30 feet above the ground, was set on fire and destroyed.

While some citizens reveled in their conquest of the desert, others grew alarmed. Among the most concerned was a wealthy Pasadena widow named Minerva Hoyt. An active gardener, Hoyt had become fascinated with desert plants

Minerva Hoyt's Desert Conservation Exhibit

after moving to Southern California from Mississippi in the 1890s. Following the deaths of her husband and infant son, the desert became an important source of solace for Hoyt. By the 1920s she was making frequent trips to Joshua Tree.

On trips to the desert, Hoyt witnessed firsthand the ecological damage being done. Worried the trend would continue, she took an active role in educating citizens about desert ecosystems. In 1927, she designed a desert conservation exhibit for the Garden Club of America's flower show in New York City. The exhibit, which featured live cacti and stuffed animals in front of painted desert scenes, won a gold medal. After the show, Hoyt donated the desert plants to the New York Botanical Gardens "to be preserved as museum pieces and where it would reach the greatest number of school children to teach them to know and to love the plants that it is now so necessary to conserve." Two years later, she designed a similar exhibit at the Royal Botanical Gardens in England.

Upon returning from England, Hoyt was elected president of the newly organized Desert Conservation League. She championed the creation of an extensive federal park encompassing parts of the Mojave and Sonoran Deserts. She was particularly enamored with the region just south of Twentynine Palms, but when Hoyt approached the National Park Service she ran into a legal and bureaucratic nightmare. The boundaries outlined in her proposal were checkered with existing mining claims and privately owned land. If a park was created, those properties would have to be purchased or accommodated. President Herbert Hoover, struggling with the Great Depression and already embroiled in a bitter land dispute with Congress, had little interest in yet another political powder keg. Hoyt's idea would have to wait.

In 1932, Franklin Roosevelt was elected President and introduced the New Deal. One of the major beneficiaries of the legislation was the National Park Service. Public works projects were encouraged as a way to create jobs and stimulate the economy, and new park proposals were welcomed. Harold Ickes, Roosevelt's Secretary of the Interior, supported a policy of setting aside land now and working out the ownership problems later. Suddenly, Hoyt found herself with the perfect opportunity to champion a federal desert park. She re-pitched her proposal to the government, and this time she received a warm reception. In 1933, the government withdrew roughly one million acres of California desert from the public domain to be considered for federal protection.

On August 10, 1936, Roosevelt signed a proclamation establishing Joshua Tree National Monument. It boasted 825,000 acres of land—less than Hoyt wanted, but an impressive accomplishment nonetheless. Hoyt's original proposal called for a park that stretched from Twentynine Palms to the Salton Sea, but the Los Angeles Metropolitan Aqueduct, which runs from the Colorado River to Los Angeles just south of current park boundaries, prevented that from happening.

Hoyt had wanted a national park, which enjoys more protections than a national monument, but the park service concluded that the area lacked any "distinctive, superlative, outstanding feature that would give it sufficient national importance to justify its establishment as a national park." The park service would one day reconsider that initial assessment. In the meantime, Joshua Tree National Monument had much bigger problems to contend with.

Although Joshua Tree National Monument existed in name, in practice its boundaries were questionable. When the monument was established, roughly 300,000 of its 825,000 acres were privately owned. In fact, there was more private property lying within the boundaries of Joshua Tree National Monument than in the rest of the National Park Service's holdings combined (excluding Hoover Dam). And the majority of privately owned land belonged to one owner: Southern Pacific Railroad. Keenly aware of the value of its real estate, the railroad stubbornly held out for the highest price.

Further complicating matters were 8,000 existing mining claims located within the new monument. Although new mining claims were prohibited, existing mines churned out substantial quantities of gold, silver, copper, and iron ore. When the monument was established, mining companies were still extracting 100 tons of ore from Joshua Tree each day. Most mines operated in remote areas, but it was no secret the government wanted them gone.

Over the following decades, the park service made small but effective strides acquiring land. They patiently negotiated trades and scoured the fine print of existing deeds to find technicalities invalidating mining claims. In a shrewd administrative maneuver, the park delayed construction of a private road to discourage private development. Then, during World War II, the government banned all gold mining in the United States due to a shortage of labor and strategic materials. Gold mines in Joshua Tree sat idle for years, and many fell into disrepair. By the time the ban was lifted, many mines had become unprofitable. Some were simply abandoned and reclaimed by the government. Slowly but surely, Joshua Tree National Monument began to take shape.

CREATING A NATIONAL PARK

A decade and a half after Joshua Tree National Monument was created in name, the National Park Service acquired enough land to turn it into a viable reality. But the monument's existence was tenuous at best. A new generation of corporate miners, armed with powerful new technologies, were eyeing the monument's vast mineral resources. Mining interests lobbied hard to exploit portions of Joshua Tree National Monument—or, better yet, do away with it entirely. Their campaign was so aggressive that some people worried the monument might be dissolved. To prevent that from happening, the park service decided to compromise.

In 1950, 280,000 acres of Joshua Tree National Monument were returned to the public domain so the land could be legally mined. For the park service, it was a reluctant transfer. But politically minded conservationists were determined to one day reclaim the land.

In 1964, Congress passed the Wilderness Act, which authorized the establishment of federally managed lands where mechanized vehicles and equipment were not permitted. Wilderness, according to the act, was an area "where the earth and its community of life are untrammeled by man, where man himself is a visitor who does not remain." Twelve years after passage of the Wilderness Act, roughly 80 percent of Joshua Tree National Monument was designated wilderness, providing an additional layer of protection. Meanwhile, a coalition of volunteers, legislators, and conservationists began discussing plans for sweeping legislation to protect vast stretches of California's desert.

California Senator Alan Cranston spearheaded the effort. In 1986, Cranston introduced a desert protection bill that would transfer several million acres of land to the National Park Service. It was hardly an easy sell. The bill ignited a fierce debate in Congress over the best way to protect California's deserts, and the debate dragged on for years. By the time the act finally reached the U.S. Senate, three different Presidents had occupied the White House, and Senator Cranston had been replaced by Dianne Feinstein. When the vote was finally held, the act squeaked through the Senate without a single vote to spare.

Bill Clinton signs the Desert Protection Act

On October 31, 1994, President Bill Clinton signed the Desert Protection Act, which transferred three million acres of land to the National Park Service. Over 230,000 acres went to Joshua Tree, which was upgraded to Joshua Tree National Park. The remaining land went to Death Valley, which was also upgraded to a national park, and the newly created Mojave National Preserve, located between Joshua Tree and Death Valley. Today, the Desert Protection Act protects the largest park and wilderness area in the lower 48 states.

When Joshua Tree became a national park, it attracted roughly 1.2 million visitors a year—a number that stayed relatively constant over the next two decades. Then, between 2013 and 2017, visitation more than doubled. Nobody except Mark Zuckerberg and hundreds of thousands of aspiring influencers knows what could have caused this unprecedented jump.

Today, Joshua Tree National Park welcomes over three million visitors each year. Its #epicbeauty, endless opportunities for outdoor recreation, and close proximity to some of the largest cities in the Southwest have all contributed to its popularity. Although peak season crowds can be frustrating, it's nice to know this exquisite landscape, long treated as a disposable wasteland, is finally getting the appreciation it deserves.

ROCK STARS & JOSHUA TREE

No band will ever be as closely identified with the Joshua tree as U2. Their 1987 album, *The Joshua Tree*, is a rock masterpiece. It sold over 20 million copies and pretty much single-handedly made the band (and the trees) world famous. That four guys from Dublin could so brilliantly capture the mythology of the American desert is, frankly, disturbing. But our hats go off to them. Lyrics on *The Joshua Tree* are full of desert imagery—desert roses, desert skies, dust clouds, thunder storms—but strangely, Joshua trees are never mentioned. In fact, U2's connection to Joshua Tree National Park is tenuous at best. The iconic Joshua tree on their album cover was actually located north of the park, closer to Death Valley. The band was originally going to call their album *The Desert Songs* or *The Two Americas*, until cover photographer Anton Corbijn told Bono about some strange plants he'd seen in the desert called Joshua trees. The next morning Bono came down with a Bible and declared that the album *had* to be called The Joshua Tree. The group drove out to the desert, located a suitable tree, and shot the cover. Bono later admitted to a friend, "it was freezing and we had to take our coats off so it would at least *look* like a desert. That's one of the reasons we look so grim." Sadly, the lone Joshua tree featured on U2's album cover has since toppled over. The location of the tree, off Route 190, is marked by rocks spelling out "U2" placed by devoted fans.

GRAM PARSONS

In 1973, the stolen corpse of country rocker Gram Parsons was smuggled into Joshua Tree National Monument and set on fire near Cap Rock. The events leading up to that incident have since become one of the classic legends of Rock n' Roll.

Parsons was a southern-bred Harvard dropout who became one of Country Music's bright young stars in the late 1960s. Many consider him to be the original alt-country crossover artist. Although his songs were country, he lived life like a rock star—flashy clothes, constant partying, heavy drinking and drug use. He became best friends with Keith Richards (Mick Jagger was supposedly extremely jealous of Gram), and the two often drove to Joshua Tree to get high, commune with nature, and scan the sky for UFOs. Before long, Gram was making regular trips to the desert.

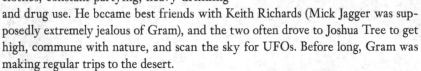

On September 19, 1973, at the age of 26, Parsons died of a lethal combination of whiskey and morphine at the Joshua Tree Inn. His body was brought to Los Angeles to be flown back to Louisiana at the request of his stepfather, who wanted a private funeral without any of Gram's friends. As Parson's body rested in the morgue, two of his friends got drunk and plotted to steal it. Parsons once mentioned that he wanted his ashes spread in Joshua Tree, and his friends were determined to fulfill his wish. They borrowed a run-down hearse, drove to LAX, and intercepted the coffin before it was loaded onto the plane. Posing as undertakers, they convinced the airport to hand over Parson's body. After their beer and Jack Daniels-filled hearse cleared airport security, they high-tailed it to Joshua Tree. When they reached a spot near Cap Rock Nature Trail (p.153), they unloaded the coffin, doused it with gasoline, and set it on fire.

In the years since Parson's death, he has developed a cult following. His story has spawned a documentary, *Fallen Angel*, and an indie film, *Grand Theft Parsons*, starring Johnny Knoxville. Musical tributes to Gram Parsons are often held in the town of Joshua Tree.

MOJAVE DESERT

✯ ✯ ✯ ✯ ✯

MOJAVE DESERT

DRIVE THROUGH THE park's Mojave Desert when the sun is low and the shadows are long, and you'll feel like you've entered a lavish dreamscape. Broad valleys elongate between crumbling mountains. Towering boulder piles rise above armies of twisted Joshua trees. Add a full moon and howling coyotes and the sensory effect is almost extraterrestrial.

The Mojave is the smallest of North America's four deserts, but it's arguably the most intriguing. Sandwiched between the high elevation Great Basin Desert to the north and the low elevation Sonoran Desert to the south, the Mojave is a transition zone with an incredible diversity of landscapes and lifeforms. And Joshua Tree's southern outpost is among its most fascinating pieces of real estate.

Joshua Tree's Mojave Desert, which lies roughly 4,000 feet above sea level, is a stark contrast to Death Valley in the northern Mojave—which, at 282 feet *below* sea level, marks the lowest, hottest point in North America. Joshua Tree's higher elevation results in a relatively cooler, wetter climate. Over thousands of years, this additional moisture has shaped the park's fabulous geology, sculpting surreal rock formations that fascinate photographers and rock climbers alike.

But look beyond the lurid shapes and you'll discover another, more subtle realm of the desert. A place where small cacti bloom in the cracks of rocks, and lizards scamper across the ground at speeds topping 20 miles per hour. A place where some plants and animals are entirely dependent upon one another for survival, while others fend each other off with deadly toxins. This is the pulse of the Mojave. It's easy to appreciate the landscape from a distance. But look close, and you'll encounter another world as captivating as any view.

Mojave Desert Hikes

MOJAVE DESERT

Joshua Tree

62

Joshua Tree
Visitor Center

Avalon Ave

Palomar Ave

Alta Loma Drive

Park Blvd

Yucca Valley

Joshua Lane

Quail Springs Road

△ Black Rock B

Covington Flats

Eureka Peak

B

Little San Bernardino Mtns.

SONORAN DESERT

△ Campground

B Backcountry Registration Board

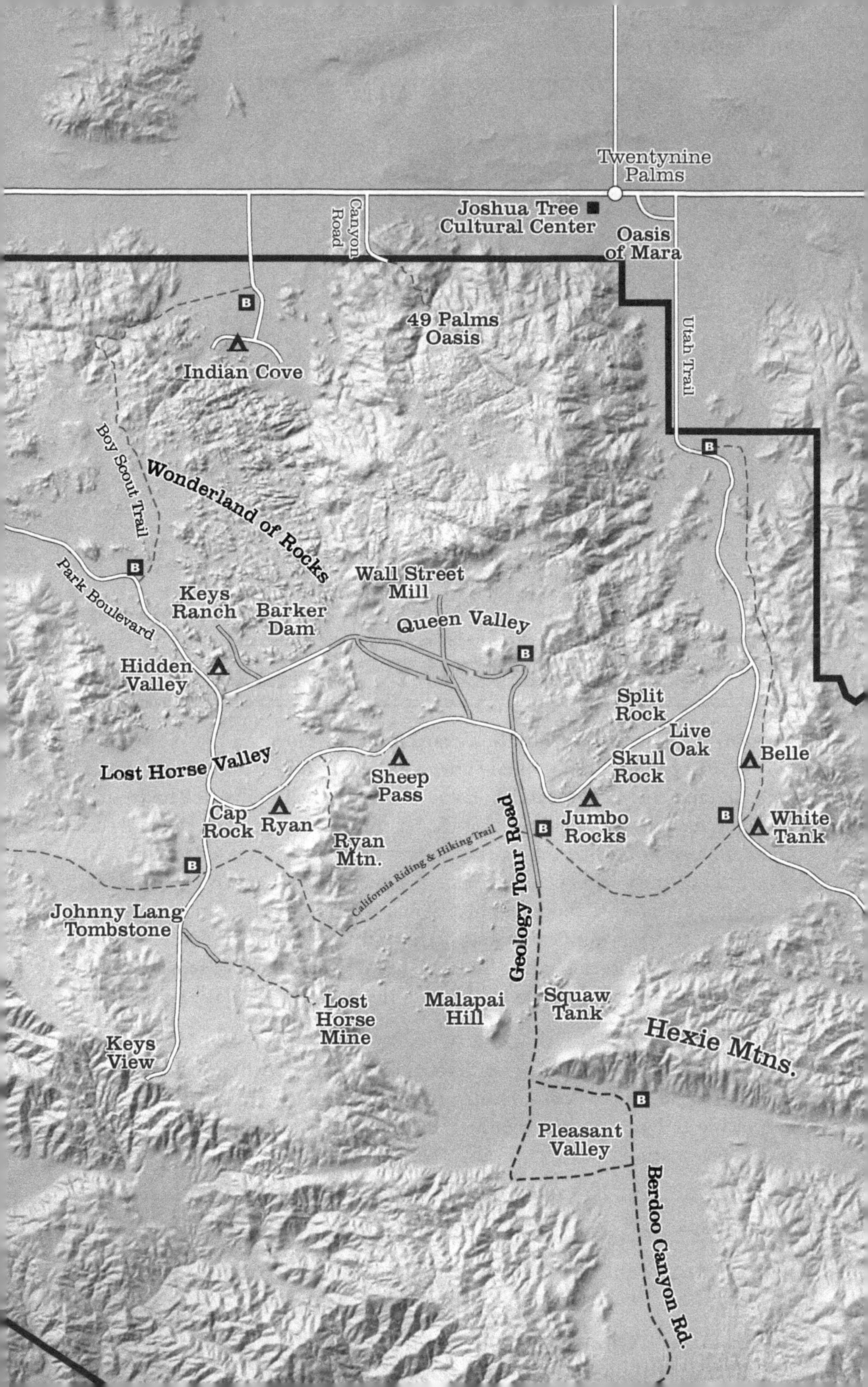

Twentynine
Palms

Joshua Tree ■
Cultural Center
Oasis
of Mara

Canyon Road

Utah Trail

49 Palms
Oasis

B
Indian Cove

Boy Scout Trail

Wonderland of Rocks

Park Boulevard

B

Keys
Ranch

Barker
Dam

Wall Street
Mill

Queen Valley

B

Hidden
Valley

Split
Rock

Live
Oak

Lost Horse Valley

Skull
Rock

Belle

Cap
Rock

Ryan

Sheep
Pass

Jumbo
Rocks

B

White
Tank

Ryan
Mtn.

California Riding & Hiking Trail

Geology Tour Road

B

Johnny Lang
Tombstone

B

Lost
Horse
Mine

Malapai
Hill

Squaw
Tank

Hexie Mtns.

Keys
View

Pleasant
Valley

B

Berdoo Canyon Rd.

⚬ BOY SCOUT TRAIL ⚬

SUMMARY Connecting Park Boulevard to Indian Cove via the Wonderland of Rocks, this popular trail is often done as a one-way hike. Hikers leave one car at the start and one car at the finish. If you start from the Keys West Backcountry Board (located next to a small parking area just off Park Boulevard), the trail runs almost entirely downhill, skirting the western edge of the Wonderland of Rocks before tucking into a series of narrow canyons, then emerging at Indian Cove. The Boy Scout Trail is the most popular overnight hike in the park. If you're planning an overnight trip, you must camp west of the trail. The land to the east of the trail (the Wonderland of Rocks) is day-use only due to the presence of sensitive wildlife such as bighorn sheep. Also be aware of the potential for flash floods when camping in washes.

TRAILHEAD There are two possible starting points for the Boy Scout Trial: the Keys West Backcountry Board, located 0.5 mile east of the Quail Springs Picnic Area, or the Indian Cove Backcountry Board, located just south of the Indian Cove Ranger Station.

TRAIL INFO

DIFFICULTY: Moderate

HIKING TIME: 4–5 Hours

DISTANCE: 8 miles, One-Way

ELEVATION CHANGE: 1,345 feet

N

BOY SCOUT TRAIL

├──────┤
1 mile

62

Twentynine Palms Highway

Indian Cove Road

Joshua Tree National Park

P

Indian Cove Campground

Wonderland of Rocks

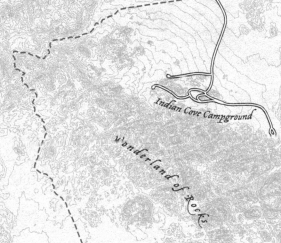

Park Boulevard

P

Keys Ranch

Wall Street Mill

Barker Dam

Hidden Valley Campground

Hidden Valley

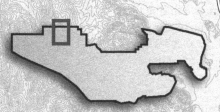

Hidden Valley

This fantastic jumble of rocks shelters a beautiful valley enclosed by towering geological formations. The easy, one-mile trail that loops around Hidden Valley might be the best nature trail in the park. The trail starts to the left of the restrooms in the parking area, then heads through a narrow passage in the rocks. This opening was blasted through the rocks by local resident Bill Keys in 1936, a few months before Joshua Tree National Monument was established. Once inside Hidden Valley, the trail wanders the inside perimeter in a counterclockwise loop. Keep your eyes out for the steely gaze of The Trojan (above), which bears an uncanny resemblance to USC's mascot. The Trojan is located on the right shortly after starting the trail.

According to local lore, Hidden Valley was once used by cattle rustlers. In the late 1800s, two outlaw brothers named Charlie and Willie Button were wandering among the boulders and discovered a narrow passage that leads to Hidden Valley. Charlie had just finished a 16-year prison sentence for double murder, and he was friends with local cattle thief Jim McHaney. Before long the Button brothers and McHaney were using the secret 55-acre valley as a hiding place for stolen cattle. Rumor has it they stole cattle in Arizona, brought them to Hidden Valley, re-branded them, and sold them to unsuspecting ranchers on the California coast. Then they stole California cattle, brought them to Hidden Valley, re-branded them, and sold them to unsuspecting Arizona ranchers. Years later, both Button brothers were killed in a barroom brawl.

Keys Ranch

For over half a century, from 1910 to 1969, this remote ranch was the home of Bill Keys, Joshua Tree's most famous white settler (p.116). A gold miner and mill operator, Keys lived, worked, and thrived here, making the most of the desert's limited resources and raising four children with his wife Frances. In its heyday Keys Ranch boasted a large garden and orchard, plus cattle, chickens, and goats. Although the ranch fell into disrepair following Keys' death, the National Park Service later restored it, and today it is listed on the National Register of Historic Places. A visit to Keys Ranch offers a fascinating glimpse into the hardscrabble lives of early Joshua Tree settlers.

Guided tours of Keys Ranch are typically offered from October through May. Cost is $10 per adult, $5 per child age 6 to 11 (children under six are admitted free). Tours are booked online at recreation.gov up to 60 days in advance. There is a maximum of 10 people per party. Keys Ranch is otherwise off limits to visitors. Directions to Keys Ranch are provided after booking a tour.

The half-mile guided walking tour lasts about 90 minutes, and the information is top-notch. From the minutia of day-to-day chores to Keys' legendary scrap collection, there's no better way to appreciate the challenge of life in the desert. The tour also includes a walk past an ancient native campsite and an early schoolhouse used by local children.

Wonderland of Rocks

As Park Boulevard enters Lost Horse Valley, it skirts the southern edge of the Wonderland of Rocks. Covering an area slightly smaller than Manhattan, this sprawling labyrinth of rock formations lures rock climbers from around the world for the quantity and quality of its climbing routes. Viewed from Lost Horse Valley to the south, the Wonderland of Rocks often looks like a solid wall of granite. But scattered throughout its interior are hidden glens, tranquil pools, and narrow slot canyons. Many locations have sphinxian names like Mystic Cove, Sneakeye Spring, and the Valley of Oh-bay-yo-yo.

The Wonderland of Rocks is one of the crown jewels of Joshua Tree National Park, but most visitors never explore it due to the rugged and confusing nature of the terrain. No established trails penetrate the heart of the Wonderland of Rocks, but two great trails can give you a taste of the jumbled, rocky scenery: the Barker Dam Loop (p.145) and the Boy Scout Trail (p.136). It's also possible to navigate the Wonderland of Rocks with a good map and compass (rock climbers do it all the time), but this option is only recommended for experienced desert hikers with strong orienteering skills. Getting lost in the Wonderland of Rocks is a dangerous and potentially life threatening experience. If you choose to explore this area, note that the entire Wonderland of Rocks is day-use only due to the presence of desert bighorn sheep.

Local lore also claims that the Wonderland of Rocks is home to Yucca Man, a large, smelly desert Sasquatch (p.41).

Barker Dam

The 1.3-mile Barker Dam Trail loops through dramatic rock canyons and pristine valleys at the southern edge of the Wonderland of Rocks. In wet years, Barker Dam retains a small, beautiful reservoir. In dry years the reservoir is sometimes nearly empty.

From Barker Dam parking area follow the trail through narrow rock formations until you reach the dam. When cattle ranchers arrived here in the late 1800s, they found a small pool where runoff collected. By damming the far end of the pool, they created a pond for thirsty cattle. These days the pond is an important source of water for wildlife, which are best viewed in the early morning. Bighorn sheep and migrating birds such as great blue herons are just some of the animals you might encounter here. From the dam, follow the trail into Piano Valley. In the 1950s, visitors placed a piano on the flat rock in the center of the valley to entertain camping groups from Palm Springs.

One of the most interesting features in Piano Valley is a rock overhang filled with ancient petroglyphs. The dramatic shapes and figures look like they could have been painted by a Hollywood movie crew—which, in fact, they were. In the 1960s, a movie shot in Joshua Tree required a scene with Indian petroglyphs. Although the filmmaker liked the authentic petroglyphs that already existed, he ordered them painted over to make them more dramatic. The crew likely added some primitive-looking designs of their own. Today the semi-faux "movie petroglyphs" are a regrettable loss of the park's ancient heritage.

Barker Dam

Wall Street Mill

This rusty, weathered mill is an excellent example of the machinery used by gold miners to process ore. Although Wall Street Mill has been idle for decades, it's one of the best-preserved mills in the park, landing it on the National Register of Historic Sites.

The history of this mill begins in 1928, when two ambitious miners struck gold nearby. They filed their claim as "Wall Street" after the nation's then-skyrocketing money machine. The name was tragically appropriate. Two years later, both the stock market and the mine were in shambles. The mine produced virtually no gold, and it was ultimately abandoned. Shortly thereafter, local resident and legendary scavenger Bill Keys claimed the land. He built a bunkhouse on the property and hauled in a two-stamp mill. For the next three decades, Keys used Wall Street Mill to process ore from other mines. Throughout the 1930s, the Great Depression lured a steady stream of men to the desert in search of gold, and there was steady demand for processed ore. Wall Street Mill could process over two tons of ore each day. Keys charged $5 a ton.

To get to Wall Street Mill, follow Barker Dam Road past Barker Dam parking area and take the next road left. The easy trail starts from the north end of the parking area. Shortly after the start, the trail forks. Turning left takes you past the remains of a crumbling house and some rusting automobiles. Continuing straight takes you to Wall Street Mill, passing an old windmill and the tombstone of Worth Bagley (p.119).

Most park visitors assume Joshua trees are cacti, but they are actually giant members of the agave family. Growing at a rate of about half an inch per year, the largest Joshua trees can reach heights of 40 feet or more.

Ryan Ranch

A few hundred yards east of Ryan Campground lie the crumbling adobe brick walls of Ryan Ranch. In 1896, Jepp and Tom Ryan homesteaded this site to take advantage of a nearby spring. The spring water was then pumped 3.5 miles south to Lost Horse Mine (p.156). During the boom years over 60 people lived and worked nearby, raising cattle at Ryan Ranch and mining gold and silver at Lost Horse Mine. An easy 0.5-mile trail heads to Ryan Ranch from a pullout on Park Boulevard just east of the Ryan Campground turnoff.

Cap Rock Nature Trail

Cap Rock Nature Trail is located to your left just after turning onto Keys View Road. Of all the nature trails in the park, this one gives you the most bang for your buck. Short? Yes. Sweet? Definitely. Easy? Exquisitely so. A flat, wheelchair-accessible trail winds through fantastic boulder formations, and interpretive signs offer scattered desert facts along the way. If you've wanted to explore some of the park's famous geological formations up close, but lack the time, energy, or ability to hike to some of the more remote examples, Cap Rock Nature Trail is a terrific option.

Cap Rock is named for the broad, flat boulder perched on top of the rock outcrop near the parking area. It's a fine example of erosion capriciously shaping the landscape. Millions of years ago, Cap Rock and the rocks below it were all part of the same mass of granite. As water eroded the granite along natural cracks, individual chunks separated and settled on top of one another. In the future, as the rocks continue to erode, Cap Rock will either topple over or wither away entirely. But many other interesting rock formations will undoubtedly replace it in the years to come.

In recent years, Cap Rock has attracted fans of late country rocker Gram Parsons. In 1973, Parsons died of a drug overdose in a motel just outside the park. His friends, fulfilling his final wishes, brought his body to Joshua Tree and set it on fire near Cap Rock (p.129).

JOHNNY LANG

JOHN LANG
DIED HERE
BURIED BY 10
KEYS TRAIL
ERECTED
EDEN MAR
25, 1925

Johnny Lang Tombstone

This lonely tombstone marks the final resting place of Johnny Lang, a shifty local prospector whose final days in Joshua Tree played out like a bumbling character from a Hollywood Western.

Lang was born in Texas in 1850, but he spent his youth as a cattle rancher in New Mexico. After his brother and six fellow cowboys were gunned down, Lang moved west, ending up at a mining camp in Joshua Tree in 1893. One fateful day Lang's horse wandered away from camp, and he followed the animal's tracks to the home of local outlaw and known cattle thief Jim McHaney. When Lang asked McHaney if he had seen his horse, McHaney looked him in the eye and explained that his horse was "no longer lost." He then told Lang to beat it.

Dejected and horseless, Lang headed to the nearby home of Frank Diebold, another struggling prospector. As the story goes, Diebold told Lang of a secret gold strike he had recently discovered but was unable to claim. Whenever Diebold tried to go anywhere near the strike, McHaney chased him away. Smelling opportunity and a chance at revenge, Lang bought the rights to the strike for $1,000 and immediately took on partners to help fend off McHaney. When the strike was registered, Lang named it "Lost Horse Claim."

Lost Horse became one of Joshua Tree's most profitable mines, producing 10,000 ounces of gold and 16,000 ounces of silver. With so much money flowing out of the mine—tens of millions of dollars at today's prices—robbery was a constant threat. The partners took great pains to disguise the 200-pound gold bricks shipped to nearby towns. Unknown to the partners, gold was stolen before it ever left the mine. Eventually, Lang's partners noticed the amount of gold produced by the night shift, supervised by Lang, was consistently smaller than gold produced during the day. Suspecting Lang was the culprit, the partners spied on the night shift and discovered Lang secretly pocketing gold.

Lang was confronted by his partners, who gave him two options: go to jail or sell his stake in the mine. Lang sold, but shortly thereafter a fault was struck and the mine ran dry. His reputation shot, Lang retired to a nearby canyon. For the next 25 years he supported himself by working a small mining claim and stealing cattle. From time to time, however, Lang sold suspiciously large quantities of gold, which lead some locals to suspect he had a secret stash left over from his days at Lost Horse Mine.

On January 25, 1925, when Lang was 75 years old, he tacked a note on his door that read, "Gone for grub. Be back soon." Three months later, his partially mummified remains were found at the site of his current grave. After setting out from his cabin with nothing more than a piece of bacon and a small sack of flour, Lang froze to death in his canvas sleeping bag on a cold winter night.

~&a LOST HORSE MINE b~

SUMMARY This nice hike takes you to the aging remains of Lost Horse Mine, one of the most productive gold mines in the history of Joshua Tree. Between 1894 and 1942, Lost Horse Mine produced over 10,000 ounces of gold and 16,000 ounces of silver—over $25 million at today's prices. The largest gold nugget the mine ever produced was roughly the size of a man's fist. During the mine's heyday a small village was established nearby, and a 10-stamp mill (above) processed the ore. The mill was powered by a steam engine, and water was pumped up the mountainside from a well 750 feet below. Today all that remains is a plugged mine shaft and the 10-stamp mill, which has fallen into disrepair. Twisting through the upper reaches of the Little San Bernardino Mountains, the trail to Lost Horse Mine follows an old abandoned mining road.

TRAILHEAD The trailhead is located at the end of Lost Horse Road, which turns off Keys View Road about two miles past Cap Rock.

TRAIL INFO

DIFFICULTY: Strenuous

HIKING TIME: 2–3 Hours

DISTANCE: 4 miles, Round-Trip

ELEVATION CHANGE: 480 feet

LOST HORSE MINE

Park Boulevard

Cap
Rock

Ryan
Campground

Ryan
Mountain

California Riding and Hiking Trail

Keys View Road

P

Lost Horse
Mine

Keys
View

1 mile

Keys View

Perched on the crest of the Little San Bernardino Mountains, Keys View offers panoramic views of Coachella Valley and the mountains beyond. A paved walkway leads to an observation area just above the parking lot. There's also a half-mile trail up the ridge to the west that takes you to an even better view from Inspiration Point—at 5,558 feet the third-highest peak in the park.

As California's coastal population spilled into the deserts, Coachella Valley became one of the fastest growing regions in the state. In the 1990s, its population increased 38 percent, more than double the state average. Coachella Valley is currently home to nearly half a million people. But the region's booming population, combined with the massive coastal population, has led to increases in haze and pollution, diminishing the views at Keys View. On clear days in decades past, visitors could see all the way to Signal Peak across the Mexican Border. Recently, however, Coachella Valley became the first urban area in Southern California to meet EPA quality goals for particulate matter, much of which has been due to successful efforts to reduce air emissions drifting in from Los Angeles Basin.

1. SALTON SEA
Larger than Lake Tahoe, 25 percent saltier than the ocean (p.160).

2. SANTA ROSA MOUNTAINS
These steep mountains rise over 8,000 feet above the Sonoran Desert.

3. SAN ANDREAS FAULT

The most notorious faultline in the world, stretching 700 miles from Southern California to the Mendocino Coast north of San Francisco (p.53).

4. PALM SPRINGS

Desert playground for the rich, the famous, and the retired. What started out as an arid refuge for tuberculosis victims at the turn of the century morphed into a Hollywood hideaway. Wealth and status followed, and before long Palm Springs developed into a world-class vacation resort and golf mecca.

5. SAN JACINTO PEAK

Southern California's second-highest peak (10,800 feet).

6. MT. SAN JACINTO STATE PARK

Located several thousand feet above Coachella Valley, this alpine wilderness is filled with pine trees, campgrounds, hiking trails, and cross-country skiing in winter. An aerial tram makes daily runs between Palm Springs and the upper reaches of the San Jacinto Mountains, rising over a vertical mile along the way.

7. SAN GORGONIO PASS

The gateway to L.A. and one of the windiest places in California (p.161).

8. SAN GORGONIO PEAK

Southern California's highest peak (11,500 feet.)

Salton Sea

At 360 square miles, the Salton Sea is North America's second-largest body of saltwater after Utah's Great Salt Lake. Although created by accident nearly a century ago, it has carved out an unlikely niche in California's ecosystem.

In 1901, engineers built the first dam on the Colorado River, helping to irrigate Southern California's fertile deserts and making it possible to grow crops year-round. But the Colorado River carries an enormous amount of sediment. In 1905, the dam silted up and the river jumped its banks. Rather than drain into the Sea of Cortez, the Colorado flowed into the desert lowlands south of Joshua Tree. It took three full years to redirect the river, and those years were some of the wettest in the history of the Colorado River Basin. By the time the river was redirected, an inland sea nearly one-third the size of Rhode Island had formed.

Interestingly, the Salton Sea had formed at least twice before in geologic history. In those cases the Colorado River jumped its banks on its own, and the Salton Sea evaporated after the river naturally redirected itself. The Salton Sea would be drying up today if not for the massive amount of agricultural runoff from the Imperial Valley to the south. This runoff, rich in nitrogen and phosphorous, has turned the Salton Sea into a smelly, briny, algae-rich soup—which makes it an ecological paradise for birds. As wetlands have disappeared along the California coast, migrating birds have found refuge at the Salton Sea, leading some bird experts to refer to this otherwise overlooked accident as a "crown jewel of avian biodiversity."

San Gorgonio Pass

This narrow notch between the Santa Rosa and San Bernardino Mountains is one of the windiest places in the United States. As the sun bakes the desert, hot air rises into the atmosphere, creating a vacuum that's filled by cool air rushing in from the coast. Much of this rushing air is blocked by tall mountains, so the surge is concentrated in a few narrow gaps. San Gorgonio Pass is one of those gaps, with wind speeds averaging 15 to 20 mph.

Starting in the early 1980s, wind energy was championed as an alternative to America's dependence on foreign oil. By 1986, over 4,000 wind turbines had been installed in San Gorgonio Pass, making it the third-largest wind farm in California. When the turbines were first installed, wind energy was much more expensive to produce than energy generated by fossil fuels. But recent advances in technology, combined with government subsidies, have since made wind energy far more price competitive. As older turbines have been replaced in San Gorgonio Pass, the total number of turbines has dropped while their energy output has nearly doubled. Today roughly 1,200 turbines deliver about 652 megawatts (MW)—about one tenth of California's total wind energy production. California is ranked sixth in the nation in wind energy production. (Texas, at 33,000 MW, is ranked first.) Although California is a leader in wind energy development, it's only ranked 17th among U.S. states in terms of total wind-energy potential.

Saddle Rock

Continue east on Park Boulevard, past Cap Rock and the turnoff to Keys View, and an unmistakable rock formation comes into view. Jutting out of Ryan Mountain's western slope, Saddle Rock is one of the largest granite domes in the park. Early settlers thought it looked like a saddle. Bleary-eyed tourists compare it to an alien spacecraft. Geologists admire the dramatic contrast between Saddle Rock's light Monzogranite and Ryan Mountain's dark Pinto gneiss. And rock climbers gravitate to Saddle Rock's towering cliffs, which offer some of the longest climbing routes in the park.

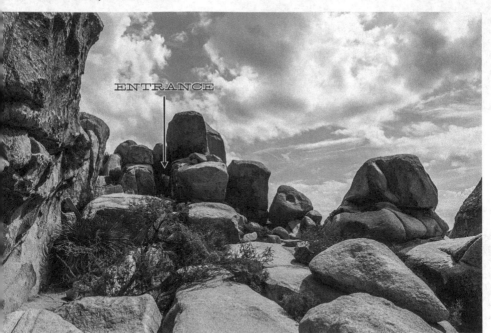

Hall of Horrors

This exquisitely narrow corridor is one of the park's most intriguing geological formations. And despite its name, it's delightful. The only horrible part is finding it. The adventure begins at Hall of Horrors parking area, located off Park Boulevard about halfway between Cap Rock and Ryan Mountain Trailhead. There is no official trail to the Hall of Horrors, but the park has delineated climbing trails that pass nearby. From the parking area, head southwest between two large rock formations, then veer right (north) around the larger formation. Head north to a third rock formation that shelters the Hall of Horrors. The well-concealed entrance is located near the rock formation's southern tip. Reaching the entrance requires some mild rock scrambling, and there's a moderate drop to reach the Hall of Horror's flat, sandy floor. Once inside you'll enjoy notably cooler temperatures, even on sweltering hot days. Enormous boulders plug the narrow skylight above. After strolling the length of the corridor and enjoying its preternatural calm, exit the same way you entered. A few yards north of the Hall of Horrors entrance lies an entrance to an even narrower corridor. Explore it if you dare!

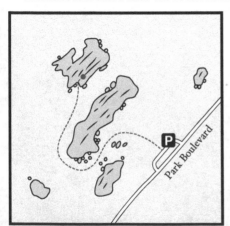

❧ RYAN MOUNTAIN ❧

SUMMARY   Rising above some of the park's most spectacular scenery, Ryan Mountain is one of Joshua Tree's best hikes. At 5,457 feet, it's the fifth highest peak in the park, but the trailhead sits at 4,480 feet, which means there's 977 feet of total elevation change. The trail starts from the Ryan Mountain parking area, merges with a trail from Sheep Pass Campground, and follows a well-traveled route to the top. The trail wraps around the craggy, northwest corner of the mountain—which offers great views of Hidden Valley and the Wonderland of Rocks—before tucking into a deep cleft as it nears the peak. Panoramic views roll down from the top, filled with broad valleys, crumbling mountains, and miles of blue sky above. On clear days the view includes San Jacinto Peak and San Gorgonio Peak, the two tallest mountains in Southern California.

TRAILHEAD   The Ryan Mountain Trail starts at the Ryan Mountain parking area, located just off Park Boulevard between Queen Valley and Lost Horse Valley at the base of Ryan Mountain.

TRAIL INFO

DIFFICULTY: Strenuous

DISTANCE: 3 miles, Round-Trip

HIKING TIME: 2–3 Hours

ELEVATION CHANGE: 977 feet

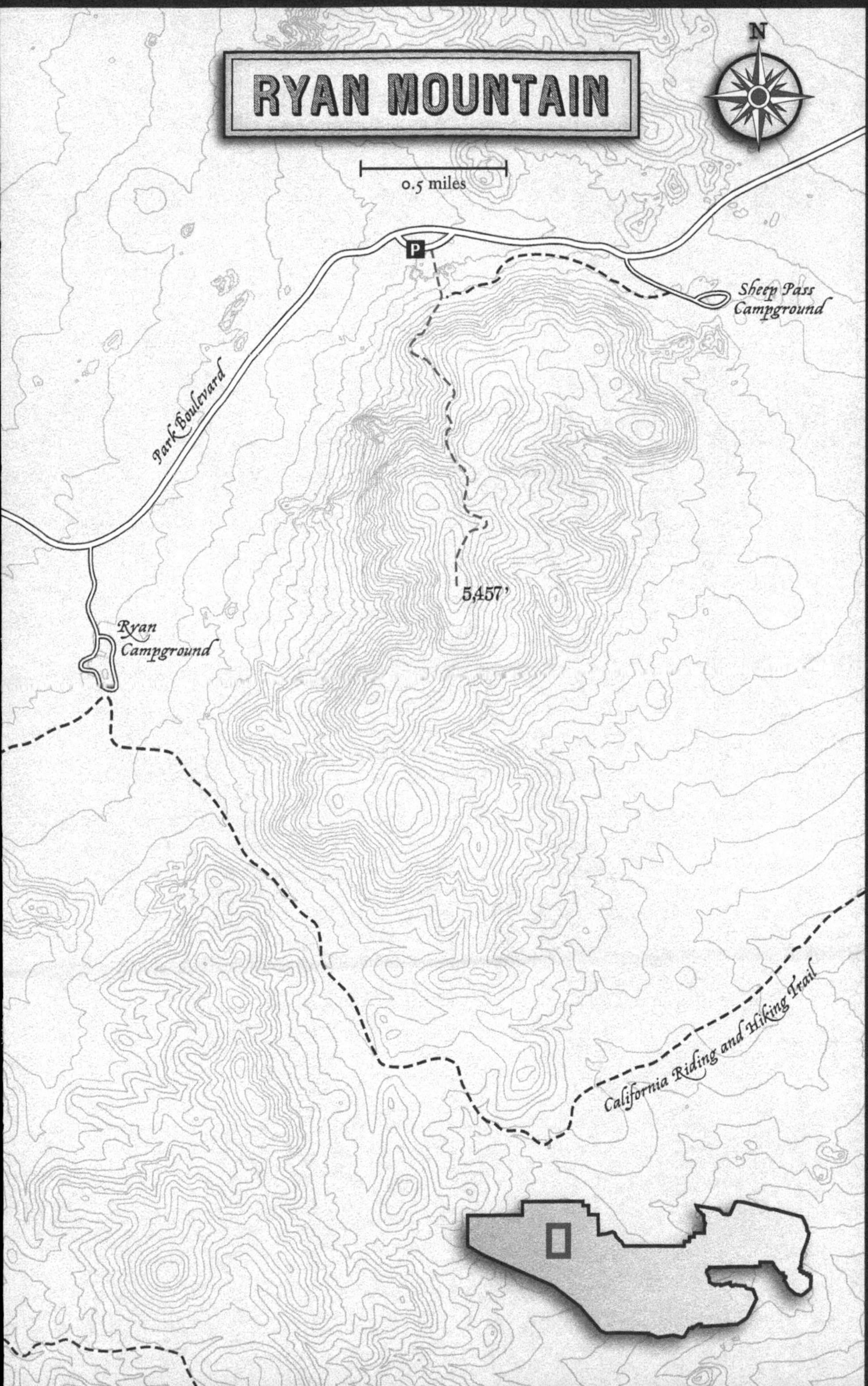

RYAN MOUNTAIN

N

0.5 miles

Park Boulevard

P

Sheep Pass
Campground

Ryan
Campground

5,457'

California Riding and Hiking Trail

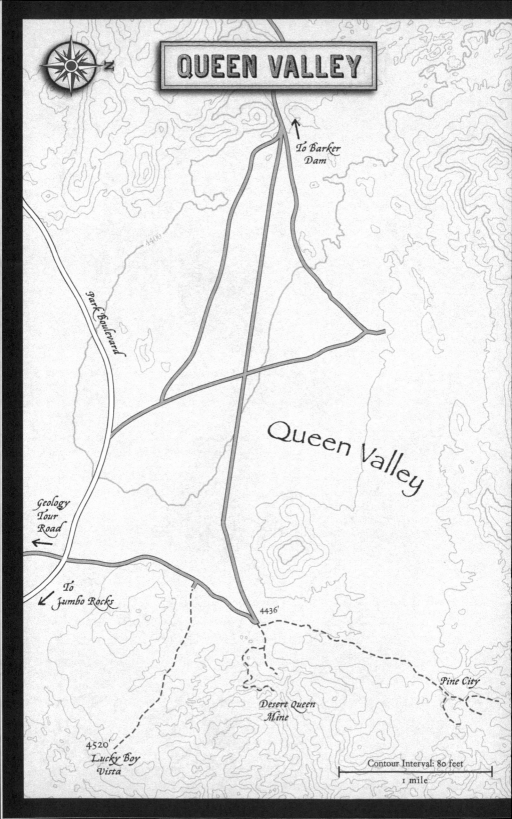

Queen Valley

The dusty dirt roads that crisscross Queen Valley are overlooked by many visitors, which is a shame because Queen Valley is home to some of the park's most impressive Joshua trees. The tallest Joshua tree in the park is found here (over 40 feet high), and there are also a handful of easy hikes, including Lucky Boy Vista (2.5 miles), Pine City (3 miles) and the Desert Queen Mine (1.2 miles).

The scattered remains of Desert Queen Mine are a slowly decaying memorial to the turbulent, often scandalous gold-mining era that flourished here a century ago. An easy trail heads to an overlook above the mine, and a slightly more adventurous trail descends into a ravine among the ruins. To get to both, follow the trail from the parking area for about half a mile until you reach a backcountry registration board. Continuing straight takes you to the overlook. Turning right leads you down into the ravine (a moderate hike).

The Desert Queen Mine traces its roots to a man named Frank L. James, who worked at the lucrative Lost Horse Mine a few miles south in the early 1880s. Determined to strike it rich on his own, James spent his nonworking hours scouring the desert for gold. In the spring of 1894, he struck a rich vein here. The deposits James discovered were described as "so rich in gold as to cause the most extravagant reports of the value of the mine," and news of his discovery spread like wildfire. Among those informed was a local outlaw named Jim McHaney, an unsuccessful miner and full-time cattle thief. On April 5, 1894, McHaney and two friends followed Frank James to his new strike, shot him dead, and took over the mine as their own.

The Desert Queen Mine produced a small fortune for McHaney, which he spent as quickly as possible. He bought diamond rings, a diamond belt buckle, a diamond encrusted hat, and a walking stick covered in diamonds. For two years McHaney pranced around the desert covered in jewels. But when the mine ran dry, his debts caught up with him. Reduced to poverty, McHaney counterfeited gold coins, a crime that landed him in San Quentin Prison.

For the next quarter century, Desert Queen Mine fell in and out of favor with local prospectors as they tried to locate new pockets of gold. The mine's final scandal came in the early 1930s, when a jeweler named Frederick Morton met a cook from a nearby mining camp who passed himself off as a skilled mining engineer. The cook convinced Morton that he could extract vast quantities of gold from Desert Queen Mine—but only if he had adequate capital. Dreaming of quick riches, Morton opened his wallet. Incredibly, the cook discovered a new deposit of gold by sheer dumb luck, but he kept this discovery a secret and pocketed the returns for himself. Morton's finances dwindled as he financed the "unprofitable" operation, and in desperation he issued illegal stock in the mine. As the story goes, Morton was convicted of fraud while the cook and his wife took an extended vacation around the world.

GEOLOGY TOUR ROAD

N

9

Live Oak

*Jumbo Rocks
Campground*

Contour Interval: 160 feet

1 mile

Geology Tour Road

4200

10

11

Hexie Mountains

3400

13

One Way

12

Pleasant Valley

14

Berdoo Canyon Rd

Little San Bernardino Mtns

Geology Tour Road

This rugged, 18-mile round-trip dirt road descends over 1,000 feet to an ancient, dry lakebed in a broad, beautiful valley. Along the way it passes some of the park's finest geological specimens: boulder outcrops, a volcanic hill, and dramatic eroding mountains. Non-geologists enjoy indigenous campsites, abandoned gold mines, and explosions of spring wildflowers following wet winters. If you're fascinated by desert geology, or simply looking to get off the beaten path, Geology Tour Road is a terrific adventure. Depending on your pace, it takes anywhere from one to three hours to explore.

The turnoff for Geology Tour Road is in Queen Valley, about two miles west of Jumbo Rocks Campground and six miles east of Ryan Campground. Toilets are located near the start of Geology Tour Road. About five miles from the start, the road becomes four-wheel drive only. Numbered signposts along the road correspond to information in a pamphlet produced by the park. The pamphlet is available at visitor centers or from a small metal box near the start of Geology Tour Road.

Note: Geology Tour Road is not appropriate for campers, trailers, and motor homes. Because the dirt road is not maintained, vehicles without four-wheel drive should only attempt the first five miles. If you do not have a four-wheel drive vehicle, do not go past Paac Küvühü'k. During rainstorms, and immediately following rainstorms, vehicles without four-wheel drive should avoid Geology Tour Road entirely.

Boulder Outcrops

As you drive along Geology Tour Road, you'll pass several massive boulder outcrops. Millions of years ago, these boulders all belonged to the same mass of granite, which was buried deep underground. As erosion removed overlying rocks, the granite came into contact with groundwater trickling down through the soil. The water eroded the granite along its cracks and separated it into jumbled chunks of rock. As erosion removed overlying soil, the rock chunks were exposed, ultimately settling into the fantastic boulder outcrops you see today.

Malapai Hill

Around 80 million years ago, magma rose under Joshua Tree and cooled to form the park's famous light-colored granite. At some point during the past 15 million years, new magma intrusions rose up under the previously formed granite and cooled into dark basalt. Malapai Hill is a remnant of this dark basalt. Geologists are unsure if the magma that formed Malapai Hill rose high enough to reach the surface. If it did, Malapai Hill is part of an ancient volcano. If not, the magma never broke the surface and simply cooled deep underground. In either case, the dark basalt is much more resistant to erosion than the surrounding light granite, which is why Malapai Hill's twin peaks loom 400 feet above the rest of the landscape.

The name "Malapai" is possibly derived from *malpai*, a word used by early Spanish explorers to describe the dark volcanic basalt flows on the southern edge of the Colorado Plateau. Malpai is derived from the Spanish words *mal* (evil) and *pais* (country).

Hikers can explore Malapai Hill up close. Keep your eyes out for Balance Rock near the hill's southern base. This giant boulder, balanced exquisitely on its tiny base, is a testament to the whimsical powers of erosion. Strong hikers can continue to the top of Malapai Hill, where 360-degree views await. Do not hike Malapai Hill on hot days, when the sun bakes the dark rocks.

Paac Küvühü'k

This rock outcrop, which has natural depressions that collect water when it rains, was long used as a gathering place by indigenous tribes. *Paac Küvühü'k* means "watering hole" in the Serrano language. Oval depressions at the base of the rocks are bedrock mortars once used by indigenous women to grind seeds with granite pestles. When white ranchers arrived, they built a dam to increase the amount of water the rocks retained. In 1919, English explorer J. Smeaton Chase described his experience at the dam: "I easily found the place, being led to it by my nose. A small quantity of slimy liquid remained, nauseous with putrefying bodies of birds, rats, and lizards."

The granite formations at Paac Küvühü'k are noteworthy for their honey-combed pockmarks. These pockmarks, called *tafoni* (p.183), are similar to the hollowed-out eye sockets at Skull Rock.

Pleasant Valley

Pleasant Valley stretches between the Hexie Mountains to the east and the Little San Bernardino Mountains to the west. At this point Geology Tour Road becomes one-way only as it wraps around a dry remnant of an ancient lakebed, called a playa. Following heavy rains, Pleasant Valley's playa often becomes muddy, then dries out and cracks into beautiful geometric shapes.

In the depths of the Ice Age, when Southern California's climate was much cooler and wetter, an ancient lake formed in Pleasant Valley. As the climate warmed, the lake dried up and dissolved salts in the water concentrated. Today the soil's high salt content is revealed by the presence of salt-tolerant vegetation.

Pleasant Valley

Gold Coin Mine

These two rusting metal tanks were once used to process ore from Gold Coin Mine, located in the hills above. The mine was discovered in 1900, and it was lucrative enough to be worked for the next 38 years. The tanks were used in a process called cyanide leaching, invented in the late 1800s and still used today. Cyanide is one of the few solutions capable of dissolving gold. It was poured over crushed ore in the tanks, and the cyanide/gold solution was then drained and chemically separated. Cyanide leaching is extremely effective. Even microscopic gold flakes can be extracted profitably from low-grade ore. But cyanide is highly toxic. Just one teaspoon of two percent cyanide solution can kill a person. As a result, cyanide's use in gold extraction is controversial. Although cyanide breaks down quickly when exposed to sunlight, accidental spills often wreak havoc on fragile ecosystems.

Berdoo Canyon Road

This rugged, unmaintained road runs 15.4 miles between Geology Tour Road and Dillon Road, located just south of the park. A high-clearance four-wheel drive vehicle is required to safely navigate Berdoo Canyon Road. The last 3.9 miles of Berdoo Canyon Road pass the ruins of Berdoo Camp, established in the 1930s by the builders of the California Aqueduct.

Skull Rock

This unusual rock formation, located just east of Jumbo Rocks Campground, is famous for its vague resemblance to a human skull. The eye sockets that give Skull Rock its eerie anthropomorphism are a geological phenomenon called *tafoni*. Centuries ago, the tafoni started out as tiny depressions in the granite. Over time, rainwater accumulated in the depressions and eroded the rock. As more rock eroded, more rainwater accumulated, leading to more erosion in a self-reinforcing cycle. Eventually, two large eye sockets formed. A 1.7-mile nature trail passes Skull Rock and loops back through Jumbo Rocks Campground. This easy trail is filled with fantastic rock scenery and dotted with signs offering assorted facts about geology and desert plants.

Live Oak

This small rest area has several picnic tables surrounded by dramatic rock formations. It's reached via a small dirt road that turns south off Park Boulevard just east of Skull Rock. The parking area is located above a gravelly wash, and just down the wash is the oak tree that gives Live Oak its name. The oak is a rare hybrid of the small turbinella oak (*Quercus turbinella*), which grows in Joshua Tree's highlands, and the valley oak (*Quercus lobata*), which is endemic to California and thrives in the Central Valley. Acorns from oak trees were an important food for tribes who lived in the park (p.105). Be sure to check out the rock formation above the oak tree, piously dubbed "The Pope's Hat."

If you follow the wash past the oak tree, you'll arrive at Ivanpah Tank. When cattle ranchers came here in the late 1800s, the most important factor affecting their success was a reliable source of water. To collect runoff, ranchers built small dams in washes, and the pools that formed were called "tanks."

Split Rock

Across the road from Live Oak is a turnoff to Split Rock, a giant boulder weighing roughly 120 tons with a sharply defined crack splitting it in two. Several picnic tables and a restroom are located near the parking area. The nearby Split Rock Trail makes a two-mile loop through fabulous rock formations.

Oasis of Mara

Located just east of downtown Twentynine Palms, this is the most accessible desert fan palm oasis in the park. A paved, half-mile trail loops through the palms, and metal signs display native artist Lewis deSoto's work *Carlota*, inspired by the Willie Boy Manhunt (p.111). An audio recording of deSoto's work is available at sandtostone.org.

The Oasis of Mara was once home to a Serrano village. *Mar-rah* is a Serrano word that means "Place of Little Springs and Much Grass." A medicine man told the tribe to go to the oasis because they would have many boy babies if they lived there. Each time a boy was born, the medicine man instructed the tribe to plant a new palm. In their first year at the oasis, the Indians planted 29 palms.

Water and natural resources at the oasis were invaluable to the Serrano. They harvested palm fruit, built shelters out of palm fronds, wove baskets out of deer-grass, and hunted animals that came to the oasis to drink. When a U.S. government expedition visited in the 1850s, they found the Serrano growing corn, beans, and squash. In 1867, the Serrano were joined by members of the Chemehuevi tribe, with whom they enjoyed peaceful relations. White miners and cattlemen arrived in the late 1800s, building houses near the oasis and sharing resources with the tribes. In 1902, a government census recorded 37 Serrano and Chemehuevi living at the Oasis of Mara. Over the following decade, however, a land dispute with Southern Pacific Railroad and growing mistrust among settlers pressured many natives to leave. By 1913, both tribes had abandoned the ancient village.

Oasis in the Desert

When precipitation falls on the mountains just south of the Oasis of Mara, it seeps underground and flows north. Eventually this subterranean river hits the Pinto Mountain Fault, where rocks and clay form a natural dam that forces water towards the surface at the Oasis of Mara. Prior to the 20th century, the oasis was a reliable source of water. But when settlers arrived they drilled wells and depleted the underground water supply. By the 1940s, water no longer bubbled to the surface at the Oasis of Mara. Today the National Park Service irrigates the oasis to keep the desert fan palms alive.

Oasis of Mara, Winter

INDIAN COVE

Twentynine Palms Highway

Joshua Tree National Park

Wonderland of Rocks

Boy Scout Trail

Group Campground

Indian Cove Campground

Ranger Station

Indian Cove Road

Rattlesnake Canyon

Canyon Road

Fortynine Palms Oasis

Indian Cove

This gorgeous campground, located along the Wonderland of Rocks near the park's northern boundary, boasts some of Joshua Tree's most impressive geology. Towering rock formations loom above the campground, a sight that's particularly dramatic while driving to Indian Cove from Highway 62. Not surprisingly, Indian Cove is extremely popular with rock climbers. Its 3,200-foot elevation is several hundred feet lower than other park campgrounds, making it slightly warmer in winter. And although Indian Cove feels relatively secluded, its close proximity to Highway 62 gives campers easy access to the nearby towns of Joshua Tree and Twentynine Palms. (See page 34 for a detailed campground map.)

Indian Cove also offers close proximity to two of the park's best hikes: 49 Palms Oasis (p.198), located just east of Indian Cove off Canyon Road, and the Boy Scout Trail (p.136), located at the backcountry board just south of Indian Cove ranger station. Indian Cove is also home to an easy 0.6-mile nature trail that loops through mellow terrain at the western end of the campground. Interpretive signs along the trail offer facts about plants, animals, and the tribes who once used this area as a seasonal camp. If you're looking for a more rugged and adventurous hike, head to Rattlesnake Canyon at the far eastern end of the campground. After scrambling up the boulder-strewn mouth of Rattlesnake Canyon, you'll reach a gorgeous slot canyon polished smooth by centuries of flash floods.

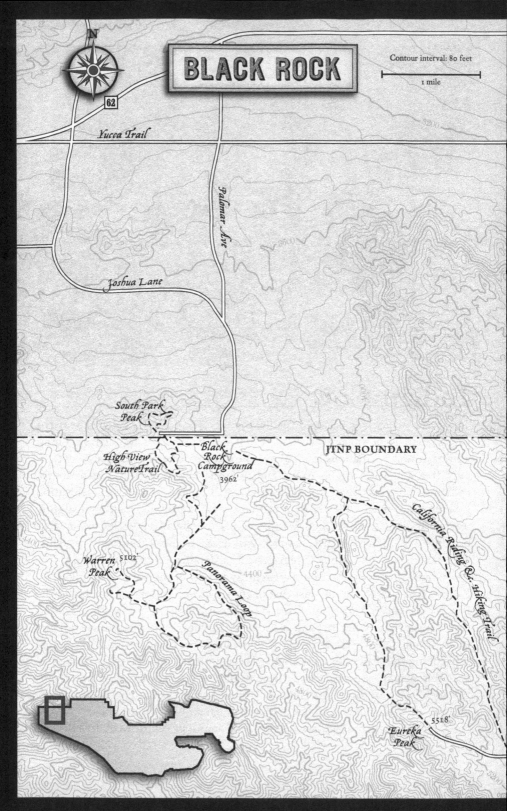

Black Rock

Black Rock Canyon, located in the far northwestern corner of the park, is home to Black Rock Nature Center, a large campground, and a handful of great hikes. This area is popular with horseback riders, and there's a large area for stock animals next to the campground. Like Indian Cove, Black Rock's close proximity to Highway 62 offers easy access to shops and restaurants just outside the park. The 100-site campground overlooks Yucca Valley, and at night the town's lights twinkle below.

Black Rock campground is filled with Joshua trees, but the higher elevations just south of the campground are filled with juniper, pinyon pine, oak, and other plants typical of the pinyon-juniper ecosystem. The vegetation gives the area a distinctly different feel from the rest of the park. It also attracts a wide variety of animals. Over 200 bird species have been identified nearby, and mule deer are sometimes spotted running alongside the trails.

Hiking trails near the campground run the gamut from easy nature trails to strenuous hikes. The easy High View Nature Trail, which starts just west of the entrance to Black Rock Campground, rambles over pretty scenery in a 1.3-mile loop. Numbered posts along the trail correspond to a brochure available at Black Rock ranger station. Adjacent to the nature trail is South Park Peak Trail, an easy 0.8-mile loop that climbs 255-feet and offers great views of the surrounding area. If you're looking for a longer, more strenuous hike, check out Warren Peak (p.194) and the Panorama Loop.

⊰ WARREN PEAK ⊱

SUMMARY   At 5,102 feet, Warren Peak is the 10th highest peak in the park. A scramble to the top provides unobstructed views of the Little San Bernardino Mountains, Coachella Valley, Mt. San Jacinto, and Mt. San Gorgonio. From the trailhead at Black Rock Campground, follow the trail a short distance, then turn left onto a service road. A short distance later turn right onto a trail, then head south (right) when the trail splits. Follow the signs to Warren Peak. Most of this hike is relatively easy. Only the final approach on the eastern ridge of Warren Peak is strenuous. If you'd like to extend the hike on your return, follow the southern loop of the Panorama Trail, which offers fantastic 360-degree views of the surrounding landscape, including (on clear days) the Salton Sea (p.160) to the southeast.

TRAILHEAD   The trail to Warren Peak starts at the southern end of Black Rock Campground, near campsite #30.

TRAIL INFO

DIFFICULTY: Strenuous

DISTANCE: 6 miles, Round-Trip

HIKING TIME: 4–5 Hours

ELEVATION CHANGE: 1,123 feet

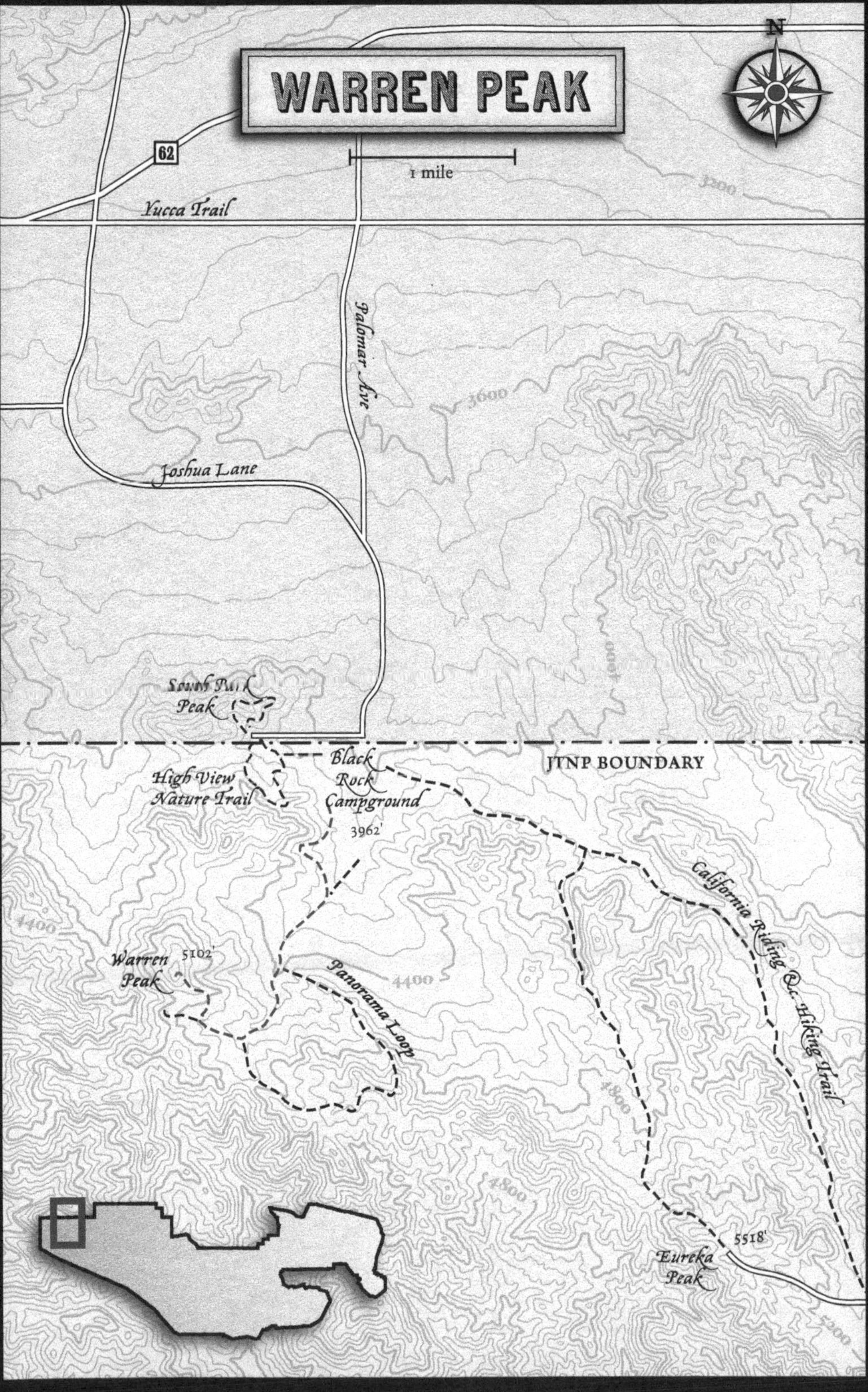

WARREN PEAK

N

62

1 mile

Yucca Trail

Palomar Ave

3600

Joshua Lane

1800

South Park Peak

High View Nature Trail

Black Rock Campground

JTNP BOUNDARY

3962'

California Riding & Hiking Trail

4400

Warren Peak

5102'

Panorama Loop

4400

4800

4800

4800

5518'

Eureka Peak

5200

COVINGTON FLATS

N

62

La Contenta

Yucca Trail

Contour interval: 200 feet

1 mile

Park Boulevard

JTNP BOUNDARY

California Riding & Hiking Trail

Lower Covington Flats

Eureka
Peak
5518

5000

5000

Upper Covington Flats

Covington Flats

The dirt roads that pass through Covington Flats provide relatively good access to a rugged and disconcertingly beautiful section of Joshua Tree. Here you'll find some of the park's largest Joshua trees, pinyon pines, and junipers. The most popular destination at Covington Flats is 5,518-foot Eureka Peak, the fourth highest peak in the park. On clear days you'll enjoy 360-degree views from Eureka Peak that stretch for miles.

Much of the landscape here is blackened and charred from a wildfire that tore through Covington Flats following a lightning strike in 1995. By the time the fire was extinguished, it burned over 5,000 acres. Roughly three-quarters of fires in Joshua Tree are caused by lightning strikes. The rest are caused by people. Fires are a healthy part of many ecosystems, but in Joshua Tree fires are much more complicated. Desert ecosystems recover very slowly from fires. The shallow root systems of many desert plants burn easily, and fires destroy seeds lying on the ground waiting to germinate. Many plants require decades to fully recover from fires. Joshua trees sometimes require hundreds of years.

Before the arrival of European settlers, fires caused by lightning strikes were part of the natural desert ecosystem. Today many non-native plants, particularly grasses, grow in the park. These new grasses burn easily and recover quickly. Park records indicate that fires have increased in number and intensity in recent years. Until this problem is studied further, the National Park Service plans on suppressing all fires within the park.

~⊲ 49 PALMS OASIS ⊳~

SUMMARY This desert fan palm oasis, nestled at the foot of a deep, rocky canyon, is one of the top destinations in the park. The trail that leads to the oasis is well-maintained, easy to follow, and filled with great views. From the trailhead it curves up and over a small rise before wrapping around several craggy hills and descending towards the oasis. Be aware that the trail to 49 Palms is open and exposed—avoid hiking here when it's hot. Upon reaching the oasis, admire the desert fan palms, which live only where there is a steady supply of water (p.68). Since the 1940s, several fires have swept through the oasis, burning away the palms' frond skirts and charring many trunks. But the palms not only survived the fires, they became healthier and more productive as a result. In addition to killing insects and other pests, the fires killed small plants that competed with the palms for water.

TRAILHEAD The trail to 49 Palms Oasis starts from a parking area at the end of Canyon Road, which heads south off Highway 62 about 1.75 miles east of Indian Cove Road.

TRAIL INFO

DIFFICULTY: Strenuous

HIKING TIME: 2–3 Hours

DISTANCE: 3 miles, Round-Trip

ELEVATION CHANGE: 360 feet

49 PALMS OASIS

0.5 miles

N

62

Twentynine Palms Highway

Canyon Road

P

Joshua Tree National Park

Fortynine
Palms
Oasis

Fortynine Palms Canyon

SONORAN DESERT

★ ★ ★ ★ ★

SONORAN DESERT

ABOUT FIVE MILES south of the Oasis of Mara, Pinto Basin Road turns off Park Boulevard and heads over a slight rise. The road drifts through a small Joshua Tree forest before dropping into a twisty canyon. At roughly 2,700 feet in elevation, the canyon yawns open to reveal a massive gulf of land below: Pinto Basin, the largest physical feature in the park.

Bounded by five mountain ranges, Pinto Basin covers roughly 200 square miles—nearly one-quarter the size of Rhode Island. It comprises roughly half of Joshua Tree National Park, but Pinto Basin is noteworthy for more than just its physical dimensions. This massive expanse of land marks one of the northwest edges of the Sonoran Desert, which stretches across Arizona, drops into Mexico, straddles the Gulf of California, and extends to the tip of the Baja Peninsula. All told, the Sonoran Desert covers 120,000 square miles.

The Sonoran Desert in Southern California is called the Colorado Desert, named for the Colorado River that marks its eastern boundary. Despite being the most arid region in North America, the Colorado Desert is home to a remarkable diversity of plants and animals. Compared with the lurid shapes in the Mojave, however, this part of the park seems barren and minimal—a stark kind of beauty that's less Dr. Seuss and more John Wayne.

This is a harsh environment that refuses to coddle its inhabitants, and they have sharpened their survival skills accordingly. I recommend you do the same. Make sure you have plenty of gas and water before driving across Pinto Basin Road, which stretches 30 miles across Pinto Basin. If possible, visit in fall, winter, or spring. Summer is brutally hot, and thunderstorms occasionally trigger dangerous flash floods.

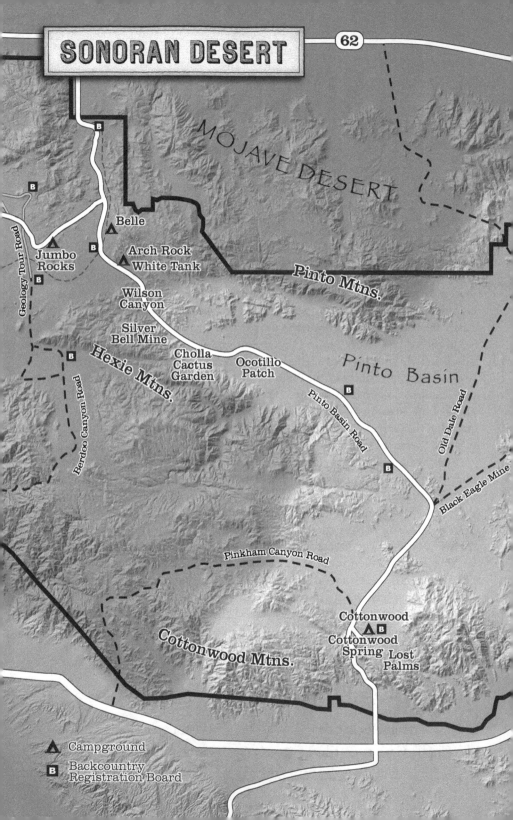

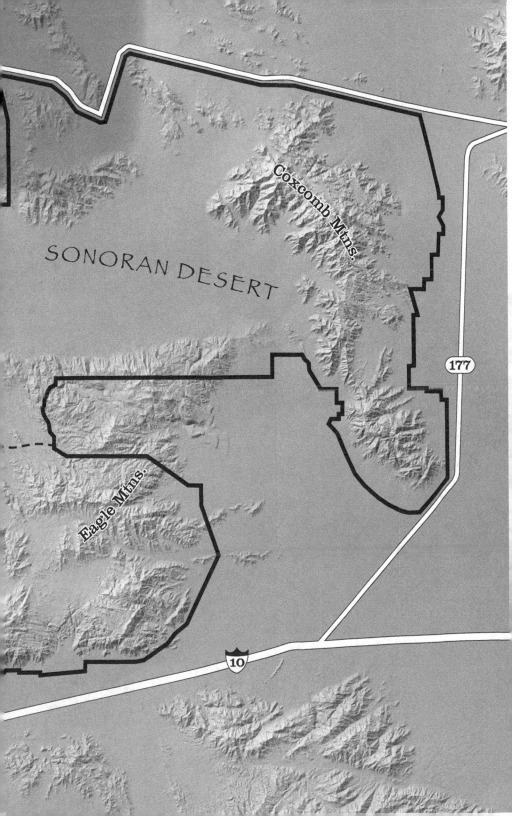

Arch Rock

This is Joshua Tree's most famous and accessible rock arch, attracting every Instagrammer who visits the park. If you're looking for #solitude, look elsewhere. Or spend some time exploring the fabulous (and overlooked) rock formations surrounding Arch Rock while waiting for the crowds to thin out. If you're visiting with kids, the rocks here offer some of the best scrambling in the park. And with a little patience, you might be able to enjoy a few moments with 25-foot Arch Rock all to yourself. Be sure to express your #gratitude.

Arch Rock is located adjacent to White Tank Campground, but parking at the campground is restricted to campers. To visit Arch Rock, park at Twin Tanks Backcountry Registration Board (aka Arch Rock Parking Area), just north of White Tank Campground. A 0.6-mile trail heads southeast from the parking area through relatively flat terrain towards White Tank Campground. The trail then intersects with a 0.2-mile loop, which passes Arch Rock and explores the surrounding scenery. Signs for "Arch Rock Nature Trail" point the way.

White Tank Campground gets its name from nearby White Tank, a water reservoir built by cattle ranchers in the early 1900s. The "White" in White Tank comes from a man named Captain White, who was involved with a nearby gold mine. When geologists first studied Joshua Tree, they started with rocks near White Tank Campground. As a result, the granite here—as well as the granite at Jumbo Rocks, Hidden Valley, and the Wonderland of Rocks—is named White Tank Quartz Monzogranite.

Silver Bell Mine

Wilson Canyon

After passing White Tank Campground, Pinto Basin Road drops into Wilson Canyon, which lies along the western edge of the Hexie Mountains. Brittle, weather-beaten hills line both sides of the road. Though stark and forbidding for much of the year, the canyon often explodes with wildflowers in spring. After passing through Wilson Canyon, you'll enter the Sonoran Desert.

The boundaries of North America's four great deserts—the Mojave, Sonoran, Great Basin, and Chihuahuan—were established by an Arizona ecologist named Forest Shreve. In the early 1900s, Shreve separated the entire North American desert into four subdivisions based on elevation, vegetation, and precipitation. He then further divided the Sonoran into seven distinct vegetative regions, including the Colorado Desert in Southern California. Because the boundaries of these great deserts are based on a combination of complex factors, they are often fuzzy and imprecise. Wilson Canyon lies in one of those fuzzy boundaries where the Mojave gradually blends into the Sonoran.

As you drop into the Sonoran Desert, you'll encounter a landscape dominated by creosote bushes with scattered patches of cholla, ocotillo, smoke trees, and palo verde. Because the Sonoran Desert is lower and hotter, spring wildflower blooms occur earlier here than other parts of the park.

Silver Bell Mine

After passing through Wilson Canyon, look for a pullout on the right side of the road with a sign offering information about Silver Bell Mine. The remains of this abandoned mine can be seen in the hills above. Look for two large wooden bins near the crest of the hills to the west. These wooden bins, called "tipples," once stored ore extracted from the mine.

Silver Bell Mine was one of nearly 300 mines that once operated within the current boundaries of the park. From the late 1800s to the mid-1900s, miners dug for gold, silver, copper, and other metals. Silver Bell Mine operated from the 1930s to the 1960s. During that time it produced over 200 ounces of gold and over 50 ounces of silver, worth nearly half a million dollars today. Silver Bell Mine also produced copper and lead.

There's no official trail to Silver Bell Mine, but it's possible to see the remains up close if you don't mind desert scrambling. After crossing over some gravelly flats, follow an old, obvious mining road to the remains of the mine. Remember: use extreme caution near abandoned mines in Joshua Tree. Many mines have open shafts that drop hundreds of feet without warning.

Pinto Basin

This enormous, 200-square-mile basin gets its name from the Pinto Mountains, which rise 2,000 feet above its eastern boundary. Early explorers named these speckled mountains after the pinto horse. The word *pinto* means "speckled" or "spotted" in Spanish.

Pinto Basin formed when the surrounding mountains uplifted along fault lines and the land between them dropped. As erosion slowly chips away at the mountains, loose debris tumbles down their slopes. Because there are no permanent rivers or streams to carry debris away, eroded debris slowly spreads over Pinto Basin, creating a broad, flat landscape. Infrequent thunderstorms wash dry, loose soil down from the mountains, creating fan-shaped sediment deposits, called alluvial fans, at the base of the mountains. As alluvial fans grow larger they sometimes merge with adjacent alluvial fans, forming long, wide bajadas.

In the depths of the Ice Age, when vast glaciers covered northern North America, Pinto Basin was a cooler, wetter place. Trees grew on the surrounding mountains, and streams tumbled down the slopes. A meandering river system flowed through Pinto Basin, supporting a remarkable collection of Pleistocene animals. Archaeologists have discovered the fossils of camels, horses, llamas, and mammoths in Pinto Basin. Giant ground sloths and saber tooth cats were also likely present. The Ice Age streams drained into prehistoric Lake Cahuilla, located

just south of present-day Joshua Tree National Park. Lake Cahuilla stretched from the Coachella Valley to Mexico and covered over 2,000 square miles—one of North America's largest lakes at the time. Starting around 20,000 years ago, earth's climate warmed and Southern California dried out. Permanent streams disappeared from Pinto Basin, and Lake Cahuilla dried up.

In the 1930s, amateur archaeologists Elizabeth and William Campbell explored Pinto Basin and discovered prehistoric objects scattered along extinct streams. The Campbells theorized that ancient humans camped along the vanished waterways when the climate was cooler and wetter. Among the most intriguing objects discovered were stone projectile points, some of which dated 8,000 years old. Thick and triangular, with notched shoulders and a broad stem, the projectile points are known Pinto Points, and the people who made them are known as the Pinto Culture. Precious little is known about the Pinto Culture, including when they arrived in Pinto Basin—and why they abandoned it several thousand years later.

While exploring Pinto Basin, Elizabeth Campbell became enchanted with the scenery. She wrote that the "great barren expanse greets the approach as an unreal valley of lavender tints ... The isolated basin reflects a quiet beauty at all times, but when sunsets turn the Coxcomb Mountains to deep rose and fills its bays and canyons with purple shadows, the Pinto Basin becomes a thing of loveliness few desert valleys can equal."

Cholla Cactus Garden

This surreal cactus patch is one of the most interesting destinations in the park. One moment you're casually driving into Pinto Basin, admiring the open scenery. The next you're surrounded by a goonish army of lanky, gangly, multicolored, fuzzy-looking cacti. To observe these bizarre plants up close, pull into the small parking area on the right side of the road. An easy 0.3-mile nature trail starts from the parking area and winds through the cacti. A fact-filled pamphlet is available in a box near the start of the trail.

Most plants have one or two common names. This cactus, *Opuntia bigelovii*, has three: Bigelow Cholla (from its scientific name), Teddybear Cholla (because it looks like a fuzzy, nightmarish teddybear), and Jumping Cholla (because its spines are so prickly they seem to jump at you). Make no mistake, this plant is vicious. The tiny barbed hooks on its spines easily penetrate flesh, and when the victim tries to pull away the cactus joint often comes with it. As the victim struggles to remove the joint, the barbed spines dig deeper. Most animals find the sharp joints terribly irritating. The desert woodrat, however, uses them to build a home. After nibbling off the barbed tips of spines, the desert woodrat piles fallen cholla joints together into a nest. Although the heavily fortified nest deters a wide range of predators, small snakes sometimes slither through the spines.

Jumping cholla are remarkable desert survivors, able to withstand air temperatures up to 138°F. Most other plants would literally cook at that temperature, but jumping cholla have evolved to withstand intense internal heat.

Ocotillo Patch

A mile and a half past Cholla Cactus Garden, Pinto Basin Road passes through a curvy stretch of road dotted with tall, spindly plants called ocotillo (*Fouquieria splendens*). Often mistaken as a type of cacti, these plants actually belong to an unusual family of Mexican trees. Ocotillo is the only member of this family found north of the border, and its range extends from Southern California into west Texas. Ocotillo can grow up to 30 feet tall on stony hillsides and alluvial plains.

Ocotillo's long, thorny branches appear dead and grey most of the year, but they flourish with bright green leaves after it rains. As soon as leaves appear, the plant photosynthesizes rapidly, storing as much energy as possible before the soil dries out. When arid conditions return, the leaves fall off and ocotillos become gray and drab once again. Ocotillo grow and drop leaves as many as eight times a year depending on rainfall. Although green leaves can grow any time of the year, brilliant red flowers only appear on the tips of its branches in spring, giving this serpentine plant a fiery touch.

Ocotillo is currently protected by law in both California and Arizona, but it was once a vital resource for people living in the desert. Early settlers' homes were sometimes built from mud-plastered ocotillo limbs. The thorny stems were also planted to make living fences that kept pests out of gardens. Native tribes used every part of the ocotillo. They burned the branches as firewood, ground the roots into a medicinal powder, and brewed tea from its red blossoms.

Pinto Mountains

The Pinto Mountains mark the northeast boundary of Pinto Basin, and they form one of the most scenic profiles in the park. Named for their multi-colored hues, which shift as light changes throughout the day, these mountains reach a maximum height of 3,983 feet on Pinto Mountain. It's possible to hike to the top of Pinto Mountain, but the trip can last over ten hours and covers long stretches of steep, rugged terrain. With over 2,000 feet of rapid elevation change, it's one of the most physically demanding hikes in the park. But for those adventurous souls willing to take it on, the sweeping views make it worthwhile.

Coxcomb & Eagle Mountains

After driving past the Pinto Mountains, you'll see the dramatic Coxcomb Mountains rising along the eastern skyline. The Coxcomb's highest point, Aqua Peak, is located 4,416 feet above sea level. Due to their remote location, few visitors ever set foot in the Coxcombs, which are part of the park's 585,000 acres of designated wilderness. In wilderness areas roads, trails, signs, and campgrounds are kept to an absolute minimum.

Continue driving south through Pinto Basin and soon the Eagle Mountains, which mark the park's southeastern boundary, rise to the east. The highest peak in the range, Eagle Mountain, lies 5,350 feet above sea level. These high elevations shelter cool ecosystems that bear little resemblance to desert below. The upper portions of the Eagle Mountains are home to isolated communities of plants and animals adapted to cooler temperatures. Ecologists call these mountain ecosystems "sky islands." Among the isolated species found in the Eagle Mountains are singleleaf pinyon pines, California junipers, scrub jays, and Merriam chipmunks. The Eagle Mountains are also home to the largest herd of bighorn sheep in the park, composed of roughly 120 individuals.

Interestingly, today's sky islands may have once been actual islands. Marble outcrops are found throughout the Eagle Mountains. Marble is limestone transformed by heat and pressure, and limestone forms in shallow tropical seas. Millions of years ago, some of the rocks that make up the Eagle Mountains likely formed in a shallow tropical sea. As tectonic plates shifted, the rocks were twisted, contorted, and elevated into the mountains you see today.

Old Dale & Black Eagle Mine Roads

This junction (6.5 miles north of Cottonwood Visitor Center) marks the start of Old Dale and Black Eagle Mine Road. These rugged, unmaintained roads once led to gold mining camps, which flourished in the 1880s. The mining camps are long gone, and today there's not much left besides a few weathered scraps. If you'd like to test the limits of your four-wheel drive vehicle, however, either road will make your mechanic very happy.

Black Eagle Mine Road crosses several washes before winding through the rugged Eagle Mountains. The first nine miles are located within the park. Outside the park a barricade blocks access to a private mine.

Old Dale Road stretches 25 miles. After crossing Pinto Basin (11 miles), it climbs a steep, rugged hill at the eastern fringe of the Pinto Mountains. It then crosses the park boundary and ends up on Highway 62, about 15 miles east of Twentynine Palms.

Desert Washes

As you drive along Pinto Basin Road, you'll see signs marking Fried Liver Wash, Porcupine Wash, and Smoke Tree Wash. A wash is a dry streambed in the desert. They are characterized by loose, sandy gravel where runoff flows when it rains. Many washes are home to beautiful trees whose deep roots reach through loose soil to underground water. Smoke trees (right), ironwood, blue palo verde, and desert willows are examples of trees growing in washes. As you drive past washes in the southern half of Pinto Basin, you'll notice distinct regions of taller, greener plants.

During heavy rains, flash floods sometimes tear through washes. First-time desert visitors are often surprised to learn flooding is a concern, but flash floods are a potentially lethal hazard. Pinto Basin provides a perfect example of how and why flash floods form. Whenever it rains, Pinto Basin acts as a massive, 200-square-mile funnel, channeling runoff into a handful of major washes. The runoff gathers with astonishing speed, and the desert's sun-baked ground and sparse vegetation do little to absorb the water or slow it down. Although Pinto Basin averages five inches of rain a year, that figure is only an average. In some years Pinto Basin gets almost no rain. In other years several inches can fall in a few hours. These violent downpours trigger flash floods that roar through washes, ripping out plants and tearing away chunks of the landscape. Although flash floods wreck havoc on existing vegetation, some desert plants actually require flash floods to reproduce. The seeds of some plants germinate only after they have been cracked open by tumbling rocks in a flash flood.

Cottonwood Spring

This roadside oasis is home to Cottonwood Visitor Center, which is a good place to use the restroom and fill up your water bottle. Inside there's an information desk and a small store. Outside there's a short nature trail. Cottonwood Campground lies just east of the visitor center, and Cottonwood Spring, which is home to a desert fan palm oasis, is located at the end of 1.2-mile Cottonwood Oasis Road.

Today Cottonwood Spring gushes over 2,000 gallons a day. In the 1960s, however, it barely trickled. The amount of water that flows here is determined by underground faults, which shift during earthquakes, raising and lowering the water level. The Cahuilla tribe visited Cottonwood Spring for centuries, drinking its refreshing water and relaxing under shady cottonwood trees. Interestingly, Cottonwood Spring's desert fan palms only appeared in the 1920s. Their seeds may have been planted by miners, or perhaps carried by coyotes or other animals.

In the 1870s, Cottonwood Spring became a vital rest stop for gold miners passing through the desert. In the days before automobiles and air conditioning, reaching Cottonwood Spring sometimes meant the difference between life or death. On the morning of July 4, 1905, a man named Matt Riley set out with a friend from Dale Mining District, 26 miles distant, hoping to reach Cottonwood Spring by sundown. By the time they left, temperatures topped 100 degrees. Extreme heat forced Riley's friend to turn around, but Riley pushed on, growing increasingly dehydrated. A few hours later, Riley collapsed. His shriveled remains were discovered just 200 yards from Cottonwood Spring. Today his gravesite lies north of Cottonwood Visitor Center.

⚜ MASTODON PEAK ⚜

SUMMARY   This dramatic peak provides sweeping views of the surrounding desert, including the Eagle Mountains, the distant San Jacinto Mountains, and (on clear days) the Salton Sea. The trail to Mastodon Peak starts at Cottonwood Spring and heads southeast for half a mile before reaching a junction. Turn left at the junction (turning right takes you to Lost Palms Oasis), and soon you'll reach the base of Mastodon Peak. A quick scramble up the peak's backside takes you to the top. Mastodon Peak was supposedly named by miners for its vague resemblance to a mastodon. If you're willing to accept that, you can probably also make out Keith Richards and Mick Jagger in the folds of the rocks. Just below Mastodon Peak are the remains of Mastodon Mine, a gold mine worked on and off throughout the 1920s. When it first opened, Mastodon Mine was extremely profitable, but miners soon struck a fault, and the gold-bearing vein was never relocated. The mine closed for good in 1932.

TRAILHEAD   The trail to Mastodon Peak starts at Cottonwood Springs and heads southeast along a well-marked trail.

◀ TRAIL INFO ▶

DIFFICULTY: Strenuous **HIKING TIME:** 2 Hours

DISTANCE: 2.5 miles, Round-Trip **ELEVATION CHANGE:** 370 feet

MASTODON PEAK

Pinto Basin Road

● Visitor
Center

▲ Cottonwood
Campground

Cottonwood
Spring
2990'

Mastodon
Peak
3440'

Lost Palms
Oasis
3100'

Contour interval: 120 feet

1 mile

⊰ LOST PALMS OASIS ᧞

SUMMARY This remote, secluded canyon is filled with over 100 California fan palms—the largest collection in the park. The trail to Lost Palms Oasis is easy to follow but virtually shadeless. Bring plenty of water on hot days. On the way to the oasis, you'll pass interesting desert plants including ocotillo, barrel cacti, and desert willows. The trail ultimately brings you to an overlook above the oasis before dropping into the canyon. The final descent, which brings you to the palms, is the most challenging part of the hike. If the 7.5-mile round-trip hike to Lost Palms isn't challenging enough, follow the canyon south an additional mile to visit Victory Palms, an even more secluded oasis. After basking in the knowledge that you're one of the few visitors to make it to Victory Palms, backtrack to Lost Palms Oasis and follow the trail back to Cottonwood Spring. Note that the entire region surrounding Lost Palms and Victory Palms is day use only due to the presence of bighorn sheep.

TRAILHEAD The trail to Lost Palms Oasis starts at Cottonwood Spring and heads southeast along a well-marked trail.

◆ TRAIL INFO ◆

DIFFICULTY: Moderate

HIKING TIME: 4–6 Hours

DISTANCE: 7.5 miles, Round-Trip

ELEVATION CHANGE: 460 feet

LOST PALMS OASIS

Pinto Basin Road

● Visitor Center

△ Cottonwood Campground

Cottonwood Spring
2990'

● Mastodon Peak
3440'

Lost Palms Oasis
X 3100'

Contour interval: 120 feet

1 mile

Desert fan palms grow over 80 feet tall and weigh up to three tons. In all of North America, there are only 158 desert fan palm oases—five of which are found in Joshua Tree National Park.

Lost Palms Oasis